IRELAND AS GAEILGE

OLGA BALAEVA

ABOUT THE AUTHOR

Olga Balaeva is an English language teacher living in Dublin. Born in Moscow in 1989, she completed a Bachelor's Degree in European Languages and Literature at Moscow State University, which was followed by a Master's Degree in English Language at Oxford University. The focus of her studies was on bilingualism in Ireland. Olga is a member of the Conradh na Gaeilge Irish language conversation group. She also holds a TEG certificate in Irish (B1) from Maynooth University. In the past Olga has written and translated articles for her parish magazine in Moscow.

IRELAND AS GAEILGE

A USER-FRIENDLY GUIDE TO THE IRISH LANGUAGE

OLGA BALAEVA

ORPEN PRESS

Published by
Orpen Press
Upper Floor, Unit K9
Greenogue Business Park
Rathcoole
Co. Dublin
Ireland

email: info@orpenpress.com
www.orpenpress.com

Paperback ISBN 978-1-78605-041-0
ePub ISBN 978-1-78605-042-7

Printed in Dublin by SPRINTprint Ltd

To Mum, with immense gratitude for her love, determination to do the best for me, constant support in all my undertakings, and understanding and encouragement of my interests, as well as for her respect for my life choices.

Acknowledgements

First of all, I would like to express my gratitude to Gerry Kelly, Eileen O'Brien, Ailbhe O'Reilly and Gráinne Killeen, as well as everyone else at Orpen Press, for making this writing project a reality and guiding me through the publishing process. I would like to especially thank Eileen for her patience and a thorough approach to editing this book.

My sincerest thanks go out to my family. I am really grateful to Brian and Gerry for being so patient and supportive, for giving up a fair bit of their free time to proofread my book and make valuable and very helpful comments. I would also like to thank Kevin for his expert advice on the intricacies of spoken Irish. I very much appreciate the moral support and faith in my abilities which Mum, Uncle and Heilén have always shown.

I would also like to thank my colleagues and friends (two very much overlapping groups of people!). I am really grateful to Bayveen O'Connell, my colleague and a fellow writer, for her readiness to encourage and give advice. Although I have kept this project pretty quiet at work, I haven't been short of support and friendship offered to me by my colleagues at the Centre of English Studies. Many thanks to everyone in the Conradh na Gaeilge's *ciorcal comhrá* for their inspiration and the opportunity to meet like-minded people, speak Irish and have fun together.

I am extremely grateful to everyone who taught me throughout the years as nothing would have been possible without the knowledge they passed on to me. Special thanks to my English teacher at school, Svetlana Murzina; to Professor Tatyana Mikhailova; and to Dr Victor Bayda, who introduced me to the Irish language and helped me to make my first steps in the field of Celtic Studies at Moscow State University. Many thanks to the staff of the Department of Irish and Celtic Studies in Trinity College Dublin who looked after me and taught me on my exchange programme in 2010. I very much appreciate the guidance of Professor Jeffrey Kallen of the Centre for Language and Communication Studies during my time in Trinity College in 2010 as well as in 2013–2016.

I am grateful to Údarás na Gaeltachta for kindly granting their permission to use a Gaeltacht map from their official website and for being very efficient and friendly throughout our correspondence.

TABLE OF CONTENTS

Table of Contents

FÁILTE

This book was inspired by two factors: the growing number of conversations I have had about Irish with those curious enough to ask, and my attachment – both professional and personal – to this language and its country. Since I started learning Irish, and especially since I moved to Ireland, more and more people from different countries – good friends, casual acquaintances and my international students – have started asking about the Irish language. It turned out that everyone already had an opinion about it but every time it proved to be more or less inaccurate. 'Is Irish very different from English? It's a dialect, isn't it?', 'Do you always speak Irish to your husband?', 'Your in-laws speak Irish, don't they?', 'It's a dead language; no one speaks it anymore', 'Sure, if they have signs in Irish, they speak it but I haven't heard a word.' And so on. Each answer started with a cautious, 'Well, not quite...'.

I admire all these people for their keen interest in this little-known language from a small island on the edge of Europe. I thought that this language and this island deserved to be known better, just as everyone interested equally deserved to be told more about them. Whether you live in Ireland, are just visiting or are interested in coming to visit one day, this book will tell you a little more about what the Irish language is, why it is so important for Ireland and, well, if it exists at all. By the way, according to the Irish Language Survey carried out in 2013, 30 per cent of Ireland's population think that Irish is a dead language.[1] When I say Ireland's population I am referring to the population of the Republic of Ireland. Throughout the book, whenever I talk about Irish in post-1922 Ireland I am describing the development of Irish in the Republic of Ireland. The history of Irish in Northern Ireland has taken a rather different course since the Republic became independent and the North remained part of the United Kingdom.

There are three parts in this book. The first two correspond to the two main questions people have often asked me about Irish. The third one rounds everything up by discussing the place of Irish in the international arena. The first part is bigger and deals with the question *Do they speak Irish?* The second one is smaller but more challenging – it answers the question *Is Irish very different from English?* See how you get on with the first one first. If by then you feel like some linguistics for amateurs, dig into the second part; there is nothing too difficult to discourage the reader. And finally, enjoy a bird's view of Irish in the last part of the book. You can find some illustrations at the end of each part – something to brighten up your reading.

---

[1] *Attitudes towards the Irish Language on the Island of Ireland* by Darmody and Daly, p. 79.

PART I

IRISH: HISTORY AND SOCIETY
(DO THEY SPEAK IT?)

The answer is both *yes* and *no* depending on what we understand by 'speaking'. If *no*, then why? If *yes,* then who does it and when? To find the answers to these questions, we will need to have a quick look at the linguistic history of Ireland and what has come out of it.

1 | THE IRISH GOLDEN AGE

The Celts, who were later to form the Irish nation, are traditionally thought to have settled in Ireland around 500 BC. They came from the continent and spoke a highly complicated Celtic language (which linguists call *Primitive* or *Old Irish*). This language gave birth to great legends, poetry and religious writing produced between the sixth and ninth centuries. This prolific period of early Irish history later received the name of the Irish Golden Age.

Some of the early examples of written Irish – Ireland's famous legends – are likely to have been composed in pagan times but written down in the seventh century or later. The earliest surviving manuscript dates back to the twelfth century and is the most important Irish legend, *Táin Bó Cúailnge*, usually refered to as the *Táin*. It is the story of a war between two Irish kingdoms for a great bull called Cúailnge. However old the story may be, the *Táin* continues to capture people's imagination today when read aloud in a pub on a dark winter's night. Other famous Irish legends include *The Children of Lir* and *Oisín in Tír na nÓg*, to name just two.

The peaceful flourishing of Irish was first disturbed when the Vikings from Scandinavia came in early 800s to plunder the country for almost two centuries. There is one thing though for which we can remember the Vikings fondly: they founded Dublin, the future capital of Ireland, in 988. The Vikings were decisively defeated in 1014 by the High King of Ireland, Brian Boru. He has become a national hero and has ever since inspired Irish parents to give his name to their boys. However, the glorious victory did not bring a long-lasting peace to the country. The darker times were just about to come.

Culture Pool

The bond with the glorious past, described in ancient Irish legends, has been maintained through centuries. The heroes of old – the young warrior Cú Chulainn and the Fianna (brave soldiers who fought together) – later became an inspiration for the generations of Irish people fighting for the freedom of their country. The modern Irish army bears the name *Fianna* Fáil, the Soldiers of Destiny, which is enscripted as 'FF' on the army's cap badge. The Irish national anthem, sung in Irish, is called 'The Soldiers' Song', *Amhrán na bhFiann*. Even one of the two main political parties of present-day Ireland calls itself *Fianna Fáil*, the Soldiers of Destiny.

2 | THE TROUBLES BEGIN

It all started in 1169 when Richard de Clare (known to history as Strongbow), a knight of King Henry II of England, was sent to Ireland to help one of the local kings to regain power. However, it was more of an excuse to invade the island. The 800-year-long colonisation of Ireland began. Ironically, King Henry II, and many of his knights, did not have much English blood in them. They were Normans – Scandinavian invaders assimilated into French society – who first had conquered Britain in 1066 and 100 years later decided to spread their influence further afield.

Up until the sixteenth century the Irish language and culture did not experience much of a foreign influence. On the contrary, the small community of Anglo-Norman colonisers began to mix with the local population, learn Irish and adopt local customs. They assimilated so much into Irish society that a seventeenth-century historian, describing this assimilation, said that the Anglo-Normans were 'more Irish than the Irish themselves'. This expression proved to be extremely successful. It was taken up by other historians and finally became a part of everyday speech. The phrase is now used to refer not only to Anglo-Normans of the Middle Ages but also to well-integrated contemporary immigrants in Ireland or Irish emigrants (for example, in the United States) who preserve their distinct Irish identity away from home.

One could argue whether complete assimilation is good or bad, but we definitely know that King Edward III was not happy about his subjects losing their Anglo-Norman identity, so he decided to intervene. At his orders, a decree known as the Statutes of Kilkenny was issued in 1367. The aim of this document was to return Anglo-Norman colonisers to their customs and keep them separate from the local Irish. Among other things, they were required to use the English language and, if they already were unable to speak it, to learn it, the punishment for not obeying the order being confiscation of their property. However, these regulations did not have the desired effect, and the assimilation of the Anglo-Normans continued until a tougher king came to power.

The situation worsened when King Henry VIII, greedy not only for new wives but also new territories, declared himself the King of Ireland as well as England in 1541. During his reign, England was in transition from Catholicism to Protestantism, whereas Ireland remained Catholic. Henry's famous daughter, Queen Elizabeth I, following in the footsteps of her father, made England officially Protestant, decisively and harshly uprooting Catholicism there. Back then, religious affiliation was of paramount political importance, as alliances were formed on the basis of denomination. Therefore, Catholic Ireland was perceived as a potential threat to Protestant England. Refusal to convert to Protestantism was seen as disloyalty to the Crown. To strengthen the position of the English monarch, Elizabeth decided to propagate Protestantism in Ireland by sending Protestant English gentry there in two major waves of migration (known as 'plantations') in 1549–1557 and 1586–1592. Her aim was to destabilise the way Ireland was run by Gaelic chieftains and put her own subjects in charge. The chieftains were dispossessed of their lands and defeated in 1601 in the famous Battle of Kinsale. They left Ireland in 1607 to bring help from elsewhere (an event known as the Flight of the Earls) but never returned; in their absence further plantations were carried out and the English order was established.

Tourist Tip

If you are interested in medieval Irish history, there are three places for you to visit in Dublin.

The Archeological section of the National Museum of Ireland (Kildare Street) holds a fascinating collection of artifacts from the Irish Golden Age. Do not miss the adorable golden ship – it is my personal favourite.

Also do not forget to see the tomb of the man who started all the Irish troubles. Strongbow is buried in Christchurch Cathedral, Dublin. If tombs are too grim for you, pop into one of the pubs opposite the cathedral and have a pint of Strongbow cider instead.

Then move on to Trinity College – the better contribution of Queen Elizabeth I to Irish history. It was founded at her order in 1592 as a Protestant university. Catholics (that is the majority of native Irish people) were prevented from studying in Trinity College until 1793, and from receiving scholarships, professorships and fellowships until 1873. Although the university-imposed restrictions were removed at this time, Catholics still could not freely become students of Trinity College: according to the rules of the Catholic Church in Ireland, they had to ask their local bishop for his permission. This so-called 'bishops' ban' was finally lifted as late as 1970.

3 | THE ENGLISH LANGUAGE CHALLENGES IRISH: IRISH WINS

The mid-sixteenth to mid-seventeeth centuries were not only a political but also a linguistic milestone in Irish history, because it was then that the leading position of the Irish language was first shaken. Most of the English settlers became landlords and formed the ruling class, making English the language of administration. As a result, ordinary people had to learn to speak it to a certain extent to be able to conduct formal affairs if they needed to. By the eighteenth century English had become the language of officialdom, whereas Irish was the everyday native language of the majority of the population. Soon, the language of landlords, the elite and social advancement became a desirable skill for many Irish people; they started sending their children to school so that they learned English.

However, the English language did not spread evenly across the country during the seventeenth and eighteenth centuries. The east and the midlands became anglicised first because most settlers were given lands there – the best lands in the country. The anglicisation of the West was going slowly though. The land was boggy and stony and not really suitable for growing anything but potatoes. So the western regions, of little interest to settlers, were left to the Irish to cultivate and survive in. The Irish language was in full flourish there in the eighteenth century, but poverty – the inevitable result of trying to survive on poor land – was growing.

The English Language Challenges Irish: Irish Loses | 4

The nineteenth century is considered to be a crucial time for the fate of the Irish language. By the end of the century, the majority of the previously Irish-speaking population had become bilingual. A sizeable proportion of people spoke no Irish at all. In the 1800s education, politics, natural disasters and people's attitudes came together to bring about the drastic decline of Irish.

In 1831 English-only national schools were introduced throughout the country. Irish-speaking pupils were not allowed to speak their native language while on school premises. They were forced to wear a wooden stick around their necks. Every word of Irish was marked with a tick on the stick. At the end of the day the ticks were counted and the pupil received the appropriate punishment.

Sometimes speaking Irish rather than English proved to be not just embarrassing or painful but fatal, as in the case of Myles Joyce, a monolingual Irish speaker from Galway. In 1882 he was falsely accused of murder and taken to court in Dublin. Neither his accusers nor defense counsel could speak Irish, so the case was heard through English. Myles's evidence, which he obviously gave in Irish, was disregarded because no one understood it or could be bothered to find someone to interpret. Without much hesitation the poor man was found guilty and hanged.

The end of the eighteenth and the beginning of the nineteenth century was also a time when a political struggle against the inferior social position of Irish Catholics began. Paradoxically, this patriotic campaign also contributed to the decline of Irish. To keep up the struggle, Irish politicians had to communicate with the British authorities and make the Irish case international, both of which meant fighting for the rights of Irish people through English.

Finally, the mid-nineteenth century brought about what is considered one of the greatest disasters to ever hit Ireland. The potato – the main element of the Irish diet – was struck by blight, which resulted in crop failures in 1845 and 1846, followed by only small crop yields in 1847 (because there were so few seed potatoes sown) and another two years of crop failures in 1848 and 1849. These events led to what is now known as the Great Famine (1845–1850). The poorest parts of the country, mainly along the western seaboard, relied solely on the potato and, as a result, were especially badly hit by the famine. These regions, inhabited mostly by Irish speakers, suffered the highest mortality rate in the country.

Nationwide, 1 million people died and a further 1.5 million emigrated to escape death as well as poverty and unemployment. Emigration continued into the twentieth century and is still a feature of Irish life, although on a much smaller scale. In fact, Ireland has never managed to recover from the losses of the Famine: the population in 1841, just before the Famine, was over 8 million people, whereas now there are only just over 6 million people living on the island of Ireland.

All these events led to the association of the Irish language with death, poverty, backwardness and unemployment. English, on the other hand, was seen as the language of education, power and hopes for a better life in Britain, America or Australia. People whose mother tongue was Irish and who had little English made sure their children were exposed to as much English as possible, including conversations at home.

The twentieth century arrived with grim prospects for the Irish language. The Famine, followed by emigration and language denial, brought the number of Irish speakers from around 4 million in 1841 to just 553,717 in 1911.[2] But could history and misfortune really have made people abandon their language?

Even if a language is disadvantaged and banned, people can still speak it at home and transmit it to their children. If they do this, the thread will never be broken because, as many scholars say, the key to keeping a language alive is using it within the family. So it seems that the socio-historical circumstances themselves could not have led to such a dramatic decline of Irish. However, the history of colonisation and subjugation did load the language with negative associations and landed the Irish in such an inferior position that they had to choose between renouncing their language in order for their families to survive, or clinging to it, knowing it could blight their future prospects. This, I think, is the biggest tragedy of the Irish people and their native tongue. It is terrible enough

---

[2] Scholars emphasise that interpreting the census data for the second part of the nineteenth century and the beginning of the twentieth century is tricky, and many factors, such as respondents' attitudes, have to be taken into consideration. For example, many people wanted to be English speakers and concealed the fact that Irish was their mother tongue. Thus, this data is indicative of a general trend rather than providing precise numbers. The statistics are taken from various census summaries for the years 1841 and 1851–1911 (see the bibliography).

that they lost their language. But it is the way they lost it that has made the experience so traumatic: they were *forced* to kill their own language with their own hands.

THE IRISH STRIKE BACK | 5

Although the Irish were losing their language, they never lost their national pride. The fight for independence in a form of uprisings had been going on for centuries before it reached its peak in the early 1900s. As the last decade of the 1800s drew to a close, discontent was growing larger and larger, which led to the formation of various nationalist groups. In their manifestos and in the minds of those involved, politics, culture and language were closely connected. Conradh na Gaeilge ('The Gaelic League') is a good example of this type of patriotic organisation. Although its main concern was promoting the Irish language and the native Irish culture, it attracted many politically active members who later on formed a military force to fight against British rule. (By the way, Conradh na Gaeilge has survived until today and is open for the public to join. Members can take part in Irish language events and attend Irish language classes, as well as visit the organisation's own bookshop and pub.)

By the beginning of the twentieth century it had become common among people with nationalist views to study Irish, go to the West of Ireland where the language was still spoken naturally or even open schools where pupils not only studied Irish as a subject but were also educated through it. A typical (in fact a leading) figure of this revival movement was Patrick Pearse, an early president of Conradh na Gaeilge (see Picture 1). He learned Irish himself, became the editor of one of the first Irish language newspapers and opened an Irish-speaking school for boys in his own house in Rathfarnham (now St Enda's Park and Pearse Museum).

People like Pearse did not, however, content themselves with Irish culture: they decided to go further and free Ireland from British colonisation and let the Gaelic language and culture flourish in the free Irish state. A rising against the British had been prepared. It was carried out in the week after Easter in 1916. This event has come to be known ever since as the Easter Rising (*Éirí Amach na Cásca*) and is of paramount importance to Irish history. The rising was defeated and all sixteen leaders (including Pearse) received a death sentence and were shot. However, the courage of those who gave up their lives for Ireland and the cruelty with which the rising was suppressed destabilised the situation. A war of independence followed which resulted in the British making concessions and ultimately withdrawing from Ireland when it gained independence in 1922.[3]

Tourist Tip

The Easter Rising of 1916 and its leaders are traditionally associated with the Irish language since they were fighting for the independence of Ireland – of which Irish is a symbol.

If you are in Dublin, go on a tour of Kilmainham Gaol where the Easter Rising leaders were shot.

---

[3] Six counties in the north of Ireland stayed within the UK and came to be known as Northern Ireland. A lot of pro-British versus pro-independence clashes have happened since but the region is still part of the UK today.

Then head to Arbour Hill across the river to see their final resting place.

In the suburb of Rathfarnham you can combine a delightful walk in St Enda's Park with a visit to Patrick Pearse's house/school and see his own letters in Irish. Finish your excursion with a lunch in the park café and enjoy a bilingual menu and Irish language learner posters on the walls (see Picture 2). The 16 bus will take you to Rathfarnham from the city centre.

6 | JUSTICE RESTORED

A completely new period both for Ireland and its language began. The newly born state, known initially as Saorstát Éireann (the Irish Free State), adopted a policy of bringing Irish back to life, with a view to making it once again the functioning language of the whole country. The initial steps to revitalise Irish had already been taken by Conradh na Gaeilge before independence. They were mainly aimed at the introduction of Irish as a subject in primary schools.

As of 1922, the Irish Free State took official responsibility for the revival of Irish. Irish was pronounced the language of the newly born country. It got its official legal status in the Constitution of 1937 (which is still in force now). Article 8 triumphantly pronounced Irish, 'the national language of the country', to be 'the first official language', while English took the place of a 'second official language'. However, this formulation reflects merely an ideal which sadly has never been achieved.

First, in the 1920s–1930s in particular, the state poured a lot of energy and effort into making this constitutional dream come true. The two main strategies used were introducing Irish into the educational and public sector, and supporting Irish-speaking regions in the west of the country.

As far as teachers' language skills allowed, the state wanted teaching to be carried out through Irish in schools throughout the country. In 1934 Irish became a compulsory exam subject. In other words, in order to receive your school Leaving Certificate you had to pass an exam in Irish. If you, a young school leaver, wanted to start a career in the civil service (that is work for the state), as of 1925 you had to pass another exam in Irish to join the ranks. Your good knowledge of the national language was a huge help if you wanted to get promoted. Bonus points for Irish were introduced in 1945. If the legal profession was your calling, Irish popped up here too. From 1929 to 2007 you had to pass an exam in Irish before you could qualify as a barrister or solicitor.

The country was divided into predominantly English-speaking and predominantly Irish-speaking areas, the latter received a collective name *the Gaeltacht*. These areas were and are situated mainly along the western seaboard, with the exception of small pockets in the middle of the country. Throughout the twentieth century the Gaeltacht has always taken a special place in the language and socioeconomic policy of the Irish state. Various linguistic and socioeconomic measures have been taken to ensure the relative prosperity of these regions, stimulate the continual use of Irish as an everyday language and prevent emigration to bigger cities or abroad. To provide this support, the governmental Department for the Irish Language, which later became the Department of the Gaeltacht, was established.

7 | THE 1960S LANGUAGE REVOLUTION

However, the push for Irish must have been too hard. People started complaining. They felt that active promotion of Irish in schools was taking its toll on the standard of their children's education. Irish was often seen as the main subject, which sometimes left other subjects neglected. Also, teachers were encouraged to teach through Irish even though children's knowledge of the language was far from ideal. On top of that, parents thought that Irish opened no opportunities in the increasingly English-speaking world beyond Ireland. At the same time, their children could not graduate from secondary school without passing an exam in Irish.

By the end of the 1960s or the beginning of the 1970s, this negative public attitude towards Irish had reached its peak. The government realised that it had to modify its policies in relation to promoting Irish. It was acknowledged for the first time since independence that the state policies had failed to make Irish the language of everyday communication throughout the country.

In 1973 came the decision that pupils did not have to sit an exam in Irish anymore to receive the Leaving Certificate. However, Irish was still a compulsory subject to study in all schools. That situation remains the same today. As a response to parents' concerns about teaching other subjects through Irish, most all-Irish schools outside the Gaeltacht were gradually eliminated.

Two years later, in 1975, it was decided that Irish was no longer compulsory for entering the civil service. However, it is still a valuable skill to have as there are a number of positions where you have to work through Irish. The bonus points for Irish lingered on for quite some time but were eventually removed in 2013.

However, when the element of compulsion disappeared, the public who genuinely supported Irish took the initiative into their own hands. A more positive attitude towards Irish started to come back from the 1980s onwards. New all-Irish schools (*gaelscoileanna*) were opening throughout the country, mainly through the efforts of parent groups. Also, both state-funded and private media projects appeared: the Irish language television channel, TG4, two radio stations and several newspapers. Everyone's right to avail of any public service in Irish, as adopted in 1936, was restated with new force by the *Official Languages Act* in 2003. In the end, Irish has become more of an available option than a compulsory way of life. The problem is that not many people go for this option.

Understandably, Irish is under a lot of pressure at the moment. Even bigger flourishing languages like Spanish or German are losing their positions in the face of English – the most widely used of the world's languages, the language of international politics and trade. Indeed how then can weakened little Irish stand against such a powerful rival, which, apart from anything else, has the status of an official language of Ireland?

8 | DO THEY SPEAK IT OR NOT, AFTER ALL?

According to the census figures from 2016,[4] 39.8 per cent of the population in the Republic of Ireland said they could speak Irish. However, only 1.7 per cent actually use Irish daily outside school. Rather surprisingly, as few as just under a third of these daily speakers (27.9 per cent) live in the Gaeltacht.

As you probably can already see, the answer to the crucial question this chapter asks depends on what we understand by *speaking* – some knowledge left over from school and rarely used on the one end of the spectrum, and practical everyday communication though Irish on the other end, with some middle ground and mixed abilities in between. Think of a foreign language you had to learn at school: this is exactly how the majority of Irish people start learning Irish. Would you say that you *speak* this foreign language now even if you have not really used it since school? I would be inclined to say no, you don't. You have some memory and some passive knowledge of it but what is needed to *speak* the language is active knowledge which allows you to communicate in this language in most everyday situations.

In the case of Irish definitely not everyone within the 39.8 per cent possesses this active knowledge. However, it is not confined to the 1.7 per cent either. To arrive at an approximate figure of those who *speak*

---

[4] *Census 2016 Summary Results, Part 1*, Central Statisics Office, pp. 66–69.

Irish on a regular basis, I analysed the more detailed census data to see what kind of Irish speakers stand behind the 39.8 per cent. A little under half of them (17.4 per cent) do use Irish in their everyday lives outside school, but not necessarily as frequently as every day. A further 12.5 per cent use it in the educational setting only. It is a limiting context of language use but I counted it in anyway: think of yourselves as foreign language students or teachers. You do not use the language with your family but it is still a language you can speak. This way we arrive at a very approximate estimation of around *30 per cent* of the population who *have the competency to use Irish and do so* in their lives in one way or another. The remaining 9.8 per cent of those who formed the 39.8 per cent are people who learned Irish at school and haven't really used it much ever since.

The pie chart in Picture 3 summarises all my calculations and explanations in a more visual and painless way.

Culture Pool

This notorious gap between the status of Irish as the national language of the country and the 1.7 per cent who actually use it on a daily basis inspired an Irish language short film called *Yu Ming Is Ainm Dom* (2003). In it, a Chinese student decides to emigrate, picks Ireland, diligently reads up on the facts and sets out to learn the country's national language before moving there. A major communication disaster haunts him throughout Dublin until he meets an older Irishman in a pub who understands what the chap is saying. The barman, astonished at the conversation between the old man and the Chinese student, whispers to a colleague: 'I didn't know old Paddy could speak Chinese!' This film is available on YouTube with English subtitles or in the Media Hub of the Irish Film Board. Once you are in the hub, you can enjoy a wide selection of Irish short films, both in Irish and in English.

WHAT'S IN A GAELTACHT? | 9

The majority of daily Irish speakers do not live in the Gaeltacht, I said in the previous chapter, and sounded unpleasantly surprised. Why? And why all this talk about the Gaeltacht anyway – Gaeltacht this, Gaeltacht that? The Gaeltacht (that is predominantly Irish-speaking areas) has always been considered the last stronghold of native Irish – more generally, a place which preserved a more traditional way of life. Ironically, though, the number of Irish speakers in the Gaeltacht has only been going down since the end of the nineteenth century. Throughout the twentieth century villagers moved to cities or emigrated, new people who were not fluent in Irish started coming into the regions, and modern technology and globalisation made Anglophone (mainly British and American) culture closer and more attractive – all this being less than helpful to Irish as a community language in the Gaeltacht.

From biggish patches on the map of Ireland of 100–150 years ago, the Gaeltacht has shrunk into very modest splashes of ink which form seven separate Gaeltachts, the strongest and biggest one being in County Galway, in the region known as Connemara. You can see all the modern Gaeltachts on the map provided by Údarás na Gaeltachta, the local authority looking after these areas (see Picture 4). At the state level the Gaeltacht is supported by the Department of Culture, Heritage and the Gaeltacht.

Still, though shrinking, the Gaeltacht stays unique in that it preserves the unbroken tradition of Irish as people's native language spoken within a community. Do all the people in the Gaeltacht speak Irish daily then? No. According to Census 2016, 32 per cent of those living in the Gaeltacht speak Irish daily outside the educational setting. Can they all speak English as well? Yes, all the Irish speakers also speak English at least as their second native language. It can be heavily accented, as a result of both immediate and historical influence of Irish, but it is still natively spoken English. Very young children who are not at school yet may be an exception and speak only Irish. It is said that there still were some people with no English in the 1970s and 1980s. For example, there is a video on YouTube of a researcher from University College Dublin recording stories told by an older man who, so they say, speaks no English. The video, which is a part of a BBC documentary, was made in 1985.[5]

However, it is unlikely that one could find such a person nowadays. There seems to be a certain fascination with monolingual Irish speakers though – go online and you will see a lot of discussions on the topic. However, the closest we can get to Irish speakers with no English is claims by people that they know or have known individuals who had 'broken' English and preferred speaking Irish.

Leaving the romatic dreams of people with no English aside, we have to face the reality: the latest prognosis for the Gaeltacht is pretty grim. Predictions have been made that if no radical measures are taken to preserve Irish there, the Gaeltacht will die out in

---

[5] Just search for 'monolingual Irish speaker'on YouTube or follow this link: www.youtube.com/watch?v=UP4nXlKJx_4.

ten to fifteen years.[6] This prognosis has given birth to extreme reactions which went viral. Someone compiled a map of the Gaeltachts where the Irish-speaking areas are dripping with blood. Another more cynical activist took this idea to its logical end, painting *RIP* on a Gaeltacht sign.

---

[6] See, for example, Ó Murchú, *More Facts about Irish*, Vol. 1, p. 67.

10 | THE ISLANDS OF LOSS AND HOPE

When you are talking about the Gaeltacht, be it with an optimistic or a pessimistic outlook, it is impossible to leave aside Ireland's many islands off the west coast, from the north all the way down to the south. Some of them have long been deserted, with neither Irish nor English being spoken there. Others have switched to English and gape there at us as a living proof of the gloomy predictions from the previous chapter. Finally, there is a third group of islands which give us hope. They are still alive and well, with people chattering away in Irish when the tourists are not listening. All the islands are stunningly beauiful and unique and deserve a chapter each. However, as it happens, some of them have become more famous than the others (as well as more accessible for visitors for transport and weather-related reasons). I am going to focus on two of such islands (strictly speaking, an island and an archipelago) in the hope of inspiring you to visit them one day. I have highlighted the islands we will be talking about on a map in the picture section (see Picture 5).

THE ISLAND OF LOSS

Remember the RIP Gaeltacht sign I was talking about? There is an island off the southwest coast of Ireland where, unfortunately, that sign could have been standing since 1953. As you land on the deserted Great Blasket, the emptiness strikes you. The village

27

ruins don't even breathe with that sense of recent life which once was. It is gone. Sheep and donkeys are still there, but untended, just wandering around with their dirty long wool hanging in tufts. The beach, once heaving with *naomhógs* coming to shore, is a refuge for seals, so quiet and uninhabited has it grown.

An Blascaod Mór, the Great Blasket, was once home to over 100 people who spoke only Irish and had very limited English (if any at all) up until the mid-twentieth century. They had their own king, they loved their language and their island, they delighted in dancing and singing, they were so alive and their culture was so rich that they attracted a number of scholars who made regular trips to the island to study the purest Irish, as they put it, as well as all the other aspects of the traditional way of life. These scholars, struck by the natural talents of the islanders, encouraged them to start writing about the island, which some of them did. The books have become classics of Irish language literature. The most famous of them is *Peig*. It is the autobiography of a woman called Peig Sayers who married a Blasket Islander and spent most of her life on the island. I said it was famous. Many Irish people would say 'infamous' and laugh uneasily if you mention *Peig* to them. This is because they had to read it at school and found it extremely drawn out and boring as they were waiting for action to happen when there was no real action to be found – just one reminiscence of a quaint way of life giving way to another.[7] You need patience for that kind of read, and maybe not a teenage kind of patience. However, if you are

---

[7] For better or worse, the younger generation managed to escape compulsory *Peig* as it was removed from the syllabus in the late 1990s.

an adult and you know what you have signed up for, why not get a copy (it is available in English now) and read about the grand quarrel over hens, or how the islanders could not get their soup when they went on pilgrimage to the mainland as they were not really able to order in English, or indeed about a fearless young man who got so cross with his mother objecting to his marriage that he left the next morning for America and was gone for years but then came back and married his faithful sweetheart. If you don't speak any Irish but would like to get a flavour of it, *Peig* is your perfect find. The English translation is quite literal, so all the sentences have that Irish twist about them.

Although of interest to scholars and Irish language enthusiasts, the Blasket Islanders were forgotten and very much left to their own devices. On the mainland, life went on, improved, was made more comfortable, but neither electricity, nor shops nor medical services were brought to the island. Looking at the village ruins now, it is difficult to believe that people in the 1950s were living in these very basic, ancient houses, constructed literally of separate stones, one upon another. It makes you realise that it was very much a ninteenth-century life lived in the twentieth century.

Young islanders started emigrating to America; with fewer children being raised on the island, the school closed. It reached a point where there was only one child living on the Great Blasket. He was called 'the loneliest boy in the world' and he received postcards and presents from children all over the world. The ageing population of the island feared that one day they would not be able to row their boats and get about fishing – the practice that sustained them. Once, a boy called Seáinín developed meningitis but the doctor could not come from the mainland because of a storm. Seáinín died. It shocked the islanders and became a kind of a wake-up call when they realised they had to leave, however sad this might have been. They petitioned the government and were evacuated in November 1953. The houses started to fall apart and grass began slowly growing in the rooms. Sheep's wool grew longer and dirtier. No Irish was heard anymore, just seagull cries. Perhaps there were ghosts at first, remnants of the life that had once been lived to the full there, but time passed and they departed. The Great Blasket is a tranquil place to be but it is also a very sad monument to how quickly life ebbs away and turns to emptiness, and how difficult it is to rebuild.

THE ISLANDS OF HOPE

However, there is light at the end of this tale, gleaming further up the western coast. Remember the fairy tale: *Once upon a time there were three bears – a big one, a middle-sized one and a small one?* Well, here is the Irish version: Once upon a time there were three islands – Inis Mór, 'the big island'; Inis Meáin, 'the middle island'; and Inis Oírr, 'the eastern island' (which is the smallest but doesn't want to admit it!). Together, they are called the Aran Islands and are located off the coast of Galway. They used to be pretty isolated and, as a result, display a more traditional way of life. With improved transport links, they have become quite a popular tourist destination. Inis Mór gets the most tourists and boasts stone walls as far as the eye can see, steep cliffs with powerful waves roaring deep down as well as ancient churches and prehistoric forts. Inis Oírr is like a miniature of Inis Mór, but instead of breath-taking cliffs it offers a sandy beach with its own moody dolphin, as well as a shipwreck and a lighthouse. Inis Meáin is a little bit left out and, as a result, is the most traditional of the three islands. It is paradise for Irish language learners eager to practise – there are hardly any tourists for the locals to shy away from.

As you might have guessed, people have traditionally spoken Irish as their first language on the Aran Islands. The islands have always had a bigger population than the Great Blasket, so they managed to survive and secure all the necessary mod cons like modern houses, electricity, the internet and airplane service, and are about to get their very own brand new branch of Supermacs (an Irish equivalent of McDonald's)!

'You speak Irish!', said the man of the house (B&B) where I was staying. I nodded. 'You are young!', he added. I was taken aback, as the second sentence seemed to have come out of the blue. It didn't though. With those mod cons, technology and increased mobility came a bit of a language change. I was told that young people are moving towards English, with all the texting, TV and computers exerting their dubious influence. Go for a stroll on the beach, or to a local café, and you will see some young mothers with their children, speaking English to them, with only a little bit of Irish inserted here and there. It makes you feel a bit sad.

Move over to the bar, though, when it is lunchtime. The 1 o'clock ferry has just arrived, half empty. All the tourists come earlier and are gone now, scattered all over the island, looking for spectacular views and those iconic donkeys. There is hardly anyone in the bar by the harbour; life has slowed down. The ferry, parked at the quay, rocks in the midday haze. The weather is nice, so the ferry crew, mostly young fellows, sit down outside to have their lunch. Take your seat with a bowl of chowder and stay quietly there, so as not to disturb the relaxed local atmosphere, and listen to beautifully spoken Irish. Or come down to the harbour in the morning, before the ferry, when the men get their horse carts and minibuses ready for the day and have a minute for a chat. Delightful Irish can be heard then. Or else just eat your breakfast quietly, and you will hear your hosts in the kitchen – they are speaking Irish amongst themselves. I wouldn't say they still speak Irish because there is some special regard for it among the islanders; it is more of a language they grew up with and are comfortable with, just a natural part of their life.

Culture Pool

Life on the Aran Islands, just like life on the Great Blasket, attracted some attention from scholars and later film-makers. A famous Irish playwright, writer and poet, John Millington Synge (1871–1909), was one of them. Over several years he spent long periods of time on the Aran Islands, studying Irish and observing local traditions. He put his observations to paper and wrote a kind of travel book called *The Aran Islands* – a slow-mover for your average modern reader but an extremely valuable read for anyone interested in the way of life on these islands.

If you are not a big reader, there is a faster and more visual way of learning what life on the Aran Islands was like at the beginning of the twentieth century – watch the 1934 film *Man of Aran* (available on YouTube). The actors are actual islanders performing their day-to-day tasks (however, it is acknowledged that the director allowed some inaccuracies and anachronisms). Those islanders who talk in the film speak very peculiar English which is difficult to understand. If you watch a later analysis of the film (*How the Myth Was Made*), you will see how a different film crew revisited the islands about forty years later. They go into a cottage looking for one of the silent boatsmen from the film. They want to talk to him but he maintains that he cannot speak English. How true it is, we do not know. He might have been reluctant to be involved or might merely have felt uncomfortable with English rather than actually not being able to speak it.

THE GAELTACHT PUZZLE | **11**

If in the middle of the twentieth century the islanders were claiming to have no English, it might seem quite the opposite to your average twenty-first-century tourist. *'I thought they spoke Irish all the time, it's a Gaeltacht!', 'Why can't I hear them speak it?', 'Why don't they speak it to me? I have learned "thank you" and "bye" and things like that.'* Well, yes, native Irish speakers and their reluctance to display their Irish are quite puzzling. Here, in this little Gaeltacht counselling section, I offer my reflections on this mystery.

Query one: Dear Olga, I want to practise my Irish when I am in the Gaeltacht but sometimes I find it difficult to get people to speak Irish to me. Why? *Irish Learner.*

Me: Dear *Irish Learner*, this advice comes from my own experience of practising Irish on Inis Mór. Irish comes naturally to native Irish speakers; it is the language they are most comfortable with. However, if it does not come naturally to you and you don't seem comfortable enough, why speak it? That seems to be the logic when you, the visitor, timidly try to utter something in Irish and sometimes find it difficult to get a response. You will really have to be brave and take the initiative. As you enter your B&B, let no word of English be exchanged; go for Irish, straight away, without hesitation. Confidence and the ability to have a conversation is what they are looking for. If you pass this test, a bond will be established – that special bond, like a fraternity feeling, that you are both in it, that is, speaking the language of these islands and indeed this country. Otherwise, if they see that your Irish is very basic, they will switch to English: a simple act of kindness – no need to strain yourself and get embarassed when speaking broken Irish if there is a perfectly suitable language for both of you to speak comfortably.

Query two: Dear Olga, I don't speak any Irish and was really looking forward to hearing some when I went on my holiday to the Gaeltacht but I heard very little. Why? *Bemused Tourist.*

Me: Dear *Bemused Tourist,* as much as Irish feels natural to its native speakers, it also seems to feel very personal. As you know yourself, when something is a personal thing to you, you want to keep it safe from the bigger world. The villages and communities people live in are so small that any stranger – Irish or non-Irish – will be spotted immediately and the necessary precautions will be taken. Our mini-bus driver on Inis Mór, for example, quickly switched off his Irish radio when we got on board. The crew on the ferry to the islands do speak Irish among themselves but lower their voices or even switch to English as if trying not to expose non-local passengers to their native tongue.

One of my bus trips from Galway into Irish-speaking Connemara is a remarkable illustration of this keeping the Irish language to oneself. Having done their business or shopping in Galway, Connemara locals gather at the bus stop waiting for the 424 to An Cheathru Rua. They keep together and either wait in what seems to me slightly tense silence or speak English to each other ('What a disappointment', I thought, having expected to hear some Irish even before I got out to Connemara). Everyone gets

35

on the bus; it is full, brimming with people and their shopping bags. The doors closed, the bus pulls out of the station, past the port and along the promenade heading west. Chatter and banter immediately fill the bus – natural chatter and banter, the atmosphere is that of relief, that of going home, and the chatter and banter is now in Irish!

I have spent several hours in the village of An Spidéal doing my photographic research, and now it is time to catch a bus back to Galway. I get on – it is warm and cosy inside, a real sense of community; the bus driver is listening to the radio in Irish, and it is loud enough for everyone to hear. Past the cottages and the moors, past the fluffy donkeys, the bus is driving out onto the coastal road heading into the city. We catch the first glimpse of Galway, and at that very moment, as we approach the city, the bus driver switches off his radio and people fall silent. We are out of the community, of the comfort zone. We are in the city (a lovely city, I must say!), but it is not the place to display the Irish language habits of the Connemara villagers. They will keep them safe and let them out when they are heading back home.

However, Irish can burst out if one is not careful enough. Three years ago, one fine Saturday evening in May, Gerry, my father-in-law, was walking down Shop Street (that is the main street) in Galway. Lots of tourists and lots of local visitors from all over the country were having a night out, many drinking. One man, definitely just out of a pub, came up to Gerry and said *Cen t-am é?* Being an able speaker of Irish, my father-in-law answered what time it was. It took the poor man a couple of seconds to realise what he had done without thinking. 'You speak good Irish', he complemented Gerry with an air of surprise in his voice. I very much doubt that our Irish speaker, had he been sober, would have used his mother tongue with a stranger in Galway City.

THE GAELTACHT HOLIDAY | 12

Despite all this mist of mystery and privacy and unspoken rules surrounding Irish in the Gaeltacht, there are the chosen ones – the visitors who get to speak and hear a fair amount of it. They are students of Irish summer colleges.

It has been a common practice for decades for Irish school children to be sent, usually for three weeks, to an Irish language summer school in the Gaeltacht in order to brush up on their Irish. Just like English language students here in Dublin (or London or anywhere else), Irish students are given a place in a host family where the *bean an tí*, literally the 'woman of the house', plays the important role of looking after the children and providing them with that extra Irish language practice. They would have Irish classes in the morning and do a number of sports activities in the afternoon, with a céilí to round off some of the evenings. A céilí is a traditional dancing session at which all the instructions for the dancers would be given in Irish. The teachers accompanying the children are meant to be very strict – should they hear a word of English from the students, off they go, back to Dublin or wherever they have come from: that is the rule of the summer school. I doubt though that it is very strictly adhered to by teachers these days.

The first trip to an Irish college usually happens in one's early or mid-teens.[8] This whole Irish college experience is not just about learning Irish, and, as the children see it, maybe is not about Irish at all. Not many of them enjoy Irish at school anyway. Forget about Irish, it is the excitement of getting away from their parents, maybe for the first time in their lives, sharing rooms with their schoolmates, learning to be more independent, and, of course, dancing at the céilí with a girl or boy they secretly fancy! Not only the céilí but the whole trip is exciting from the boys' and girls' perspective. Some children would have gone to single-sex primary schools, many of them might be also going to a single-sex secondary school at the time. So that trip to the Galetacht is a time when girls and boys get to study and do sport and other activities together, which could be a novelty for some students and a source of excitement for everyone. Hopefully, busy though they are with all that stuff going on, they learn some Irish too.

Some of those school children will return to Irish colleges in a little while. This time they will be on the opposite side of the barricade though: no longer school children but aspiring primary school teachers. As you will soon learn from the School Irish chapter (Chapter 14), every primary school teacher has to study for three weeks in the Gaeltacht before they qualify. On this kind of trip there is more focus on Irish, I guess, and fewer hormones at play. Though, you never know.

---

[8] It is possible to go later too, say, when you are seventeen or eighteen, to get ready for the Leaving Certificate exams. However, the tendency is for the children to go to an Irish college when they are fourteen to sixteen years old.

Culture Pool

The Irish college experience, so familiar to most Irish people, and yet so unique, has become the topic of the novel *The Dancers Dancing* by Éilís Ní Dhuibhne. The book is a very special combination of universal and very Irish themes. All so recognisable emotions and worries of a teenage girl are placed against the backdrop of an Irish college in the Gaeltacht in the summer of 1972. The novel digs deeper than your average teenage fiction though. We are presented with the public perception of Irish and the Gaeltacht through the eyes of the main heroine. The east and west of Ireland, the imagined and the reality, complex Irish identities – all these themes are masterfully woven into the narrative. It is a great read with an insight into the Irish life. You might need to look up a couple of Irish phrases which are used in the text without translation, but Google is always there for you.

13 | TO KEEP OR NOT TO KEEP?

The spectrum of opinions is vast: from those who are extremely passionate about the language, through the middle ground of indifference, to fierce dislike. I have met people of all three categories, the middle one prevailing. When asked, 70 per cent of the population agreed that the majority of people simply don't care about Irish.[9] However, the general mood in the country is quite optimistic, with 67 per cent of the population feeling positive about Irish. The majority (64 per cent) also think that Ireland would lose its cultural identity without its indigenous language.

There is, however, a darker side to this fairly bright and hopeful picture: whereas so many people think that the existence of Irish is essential, only half of them (30.3 per cent)[10] use it in one way or another. The rest are not that willing to turn their emotional support into action. Professor B. Ó Doibhlin, in the book *Who Needs Irish?*, makes an apt comparison to describe this widespread attitude to Irish: 'There it is like some toothless grandmother huddled by our hearth. ... We can't in all decency throw her out – she is after all of our blood – but we can park her in a geriatric ghetto where she can

---

[9]   Unless otherwise stated, the attitude statistics used in this section come from the official report *Attitudes towards the Irish Language on the Island of Ireland* by Darmody and Daly. It summarises data from Irish language surveys in 2001 and 2013. Only data for the Republic of Ireland is quoted here.
[10]   *Census 2016 Summary Results, Part 1*, p. 67.

expire in comfort and in solitude, while we get on with the business of living'.[11]

This tendency to passively support Irish just above the level of survival is reflected in adults' attitude to the presence of Irish at school: 82 per cent of adults agree that all children in the country should learn Irish, while a very sizable proportion (43 per cent) think that Irish is more important than another foreign language at school (in my opinion, so many people agree with this statement because their children already know the most important language in the modern world). However, when it again comes to taking one step further, the statistics change. The majority do not want their children to be taught through Irish; they prefer to see it only as a subject. When asked about their vision of Ireland in the future, most people agreed on a bilingual Ireland with English as its main language.

---

[11]   'An Enterprise of the Spirit' by Ó Doibhlin, p. 145.

14 | SCHOOL IRISH: A SEPARATE CHAPTER

As you have seen, it is not rare for people to have opinions about the place of Irish at school and how much Irish their children should learn. However, for many children, school is not the first place where they start learning Irish. Busy parents send their three-, four- and five-year-olds to pre-schools where they socialise and learn through play. Many pre-school teachers introduce the kids to Irish. They teach them everyday words and expressions and sing songs in Irish. If parents are feeling super ambitious, they send their children to Irish-speaking pre-schools called *naíonraí*, where everything happens through Irish.

Next comes school, and there is no hiding from Irish here. It has been a compulsory subject since the early 1930s. When the preparation time for the Leaving Certificate (i.e. final) exams comes, students choose six subjects to study. They are free to pick three; the other three have long been chosen for them: Maths, English, and, yes, you guessed it, Irish. Every so often, around the time of the Leaving Certificate exams, polemical articles and a string of readers' passionate comments flare up in the national newspapers and on various forums: *Forcing students to study Irish is a disgrace!*[12] Or: *Irish is the native language of Ireland; there's no*

---

[12] Paraphrased from Rosita Boland: 'Broadside: Can Anybody Truthfully Say that Irish Is a Necessary Language?', *Irish Times*, 30 May 2016.

way we can give up teaching it.[13] Or: *Shouldn't we spend taxpayers' money on something more practical?*[14] And so on and so forth. There is no end in sight.

However, if you (or your parents) are not fans of Irish, you might get lucky and be exempt from studying it at school if you can satisfy certain conditions. Are you a foreign national? Have you lived abroad before moving back to Ireland? Or maybe you have learning difficulties recognised by a mental health professional? If you tick any of these boxes, then you might be off the hook. Don't be in a hurry to renounce Irish though. Despite all the talk, there are some real practical benefits to studying Irish and studying it hard. For those brave souls who not only study Irish but decide to do all their Leaving Certificate exams through Irish (Maths, Geography, whatever it is), a well-deserved reward has been prepared: they get extra points on top of their exam marks, which means they have more chances of getting into the university course of their choice.

And it is not only school students who have to work hard. All primary school teachers have to be able to speak Irish competently because they will be teaching it to kids alongside all the other subjects. Even before they start their teacher training course future teachers have to pass an interview in Irish and then study it to quite a high standard, spend three weeks practising it in the Gaeltacht and sit exams at the end of it all. Those primary school teachers who qualified outside Ireland (usually in the UK) and want to come and teach in Ireland have a bit of a problem. Their qualification will not be fully

---

[13] Paraphrased from Eugene Reavey: 'Head-To-Head: The Irish Language Debate', *University Times*, 21 February 2011.
[14] Various sources, including opinions which people have expressed to me in private conversation.

recognised until they have passed the four necessary exams in Irish and have been to the Gaeltacht.

As a result, many teachers in training (or re-training) get worried about their Irish and go back to Irish classes or join Irish conversation groups. Whenever you turn up at a Conradh na Gaeilge conversation group I can almost certainly guarantee that you will meet a primary school teacher or someone in training. And usually more than one. Secondary school teachers are not that much under pressure: they have to know only one subject. If it happens to be Irish, it is most likely that they are already fluent as they are expected to have a degree in their chosen subject.

The teachers with most Irish, however, tend to be those who teach in a very special type of school: *gaelscoilenna*, that is Irish-medium schools. These schools teach all subjects through Irish. When people say 'gaelscoileanna' they mean Irish-medium schools outside the Gaeltacht. Obviously, they exist in the Gaeltacht too but they are more mainstream there and have been operating for longer. As for the rest of the country, gaelscoileanna are a relatively recent phenomenon. The movement to establish Irish-medium schools throughout the country started in the early 1970s. Ordinary people – parents and Irish language enthusiasts – have traditionally been behind each new school project. The state appreciates people's commitement to Irish and offers some funding for such schools. It has been fifty years since the movement started and gaelscoileanna are far from going out of fashion. Their number has only been growing ever since. As of 2016/2017, there are 145 primary and 44 secondary gaelscoileanna[15] (compare this to the 1972

---

[15]   Figures provided by www.gaelscoileanna.ie.

figures of 11 and 5 respectively), and this is still not enough. They say that if you want your child to go to a gaelscoil, you had better sign them up once they are born! (I am not joking, several years' queues are real.)

Why are people so enthusiastic, you will ask? Has everyone suddenly gone crazy about Irish? Sounds a bit suspicious, you will say. Maybe. There is definitely an increase in the number of people who are interested in Irish, and even if they do not speak it well, they want their children to do so. In some cases, having a child attend a gaelscoil becomes a learning experience for the whole family, as his parents have to brush up on their Irish before helping him with his *obair bhaile* (homework). However, you were right, there is a more pragmatic side to it all. Over time, gaelscoileanna have earned a reputation as schools with high stand-ards and, as a result, better academic performance in students. Sometimes you would have a situation when parents are attracted by this side of gaeilscoile-anna rather than the desire to educate their children through Irish. This, in turn, has brought some criticism of gaelscoileanna as well as those who choose them for their children. Some people view gaelscoileanna as elitist, mainly middle-class schools where snobbish parents send their children to make sure they mix only with highly motivated kids from the same background.

Whatever the reasons for going to a gaelscoil might be, one thing is certain – their graduates are normally more confident about speaking Irish, are more willing to do so and complain less about 'the painful yet useless' experience of studying the language for thirteen long years. Ordinary mortals, however, agree that learning Irish at school was an unpleasant experience. 'I hated it', says my husband, who is now eager to re-learn the language. 'You see, the problem is that they teach it so badly at school', says a middle-aged woman from my Irish class. Most people associate learning Irish at school with strict teachers, confusion over complex grammar, boredom and, as a result, a feeling that Irish classes are both painful and pointless. Most people agree that they had spent thirteen years doing Irish at school, did not learn anything and disliked the experience. It seems to me sometimes that a bad experience with Irish at school has become something of a must-have. If it is Irish and school, your experience is almost expected to be negative.

Cecilia Ahern, in her novel *The Marble Collector*, describes how miserable Fergus, the main character, is at his new school. Have you guessed why? Yes, he is in his Irish lesson, and the priest is shouting in Irish, and the boy does not understand him but is required to recite basic grammar forms. So widespread and familiar is the disillusionment with school Irish that the tourism industry touched on it in the *You are 100% Irish when...* series of T-shirts and other merchindise. The T-shirt in Picture 6 makes fun of the amount of Irish with which most people enter adult life. It is the case in many schools that certain set phrases for daily routines must be exchanged in Irish – for example, when a pupil asks for permission to go to the bathroom: *An bhfuil cead agam dul go dtí an leithreas?* This vital request, the T-shirt tells us, is the longest Irish phrase most Irish pupils remember after school. However humble your school Irish is, it can still come in useful should you choose to head for the Gaeltacht and try out those hard-learned phrases with the locals.

How to Be 100% Irish | 15

The significance of these Gaeltacht trips goes well beyond practising Irish, experiencing freedom from your parents and getting your first kiss. What happens in the Gaeltacht stays in your mind. The Irish language, traditional dancing, music and sport, witnessed in the Gaeltacht, often become ways of expressing people's Irishness in their adult life.

For many people, both active and passive speakers, Irish is a symbol of Irish national identity. When they need to emphasise their Irishness, people may appeal to Irish even if they only rarely speak it or don't speak it at all. As noticed by researchers and laypeople alike, Irish people start using basic Irish among themselves when they go abroad. It can be done to gossip about the people around them. Or else they would switch to Irish just for a minute or two, to make sure that the international crowd at the pool in Mallorca do not confuse them with the Brits. All most Irish people would use is a little bit of school Irish or, as in one story I heard from my colleagues, random phrases they can remember: the notorious *An bhfuil cead agam dul go dtí an leithreas?* repeated over and over again and interpersed with 'Thank you', 'Cheers', 'I live in …' and so on. Anything goes when national pride is at stake!

Indeed, national pride and Irish often go hand in hand, even in brief encounters like my recent one with a plumber who came to fix my tap. As he was getting ready to go, he asked me how to say 'Goodbye' in Russian, my mother tongue. I told him, he repeated it and then, as he was leaving, after the English exchange of 'Goodbyes' and 'Thanks', he said *Slán*, which is 'Goodbye' in Irish. This is remarkable: our converstion was a kind of a cultural exchange between the two nations. He asked me something about my mother tongue and then felt he had to share his with me. What he shared was Irish, although the chance that this man was a native Irish speaker is very small.[16]

The ultimate official manifestation of one's national identity is the national anthem. And, guess what, the Irish national anthem is sung in Irish. It is called *Amhrán na Bhfiann* ('The Soldiers' Song'). Originally written in English in 1907, it was a rebel song used by those fighting for Ireland's independece from Britain. After the establishement of the Free State, it was trans-lated into Irish in 1923 by Liam Ó Rinn and officially became the national anthem in 1926. Ironically and sadly, learning the national anthem by heart turned out to be a bit of a struggle for many. Most ordinary people have a good chance of getting through their lives without knowing the anthem word for word, with no one knowing about their not knowing it (or suspecting but never bringing it up). It is the football players who get all the scoffing. The national anthem at the start of a match may be as anticipated as the match itself. Not because the viewers are overly keen or are going to sing along. They are waiting for that awkward moment of truth when a close-up of every footballer comes up

---

[16] You might argue that there was no way he would teach me 'Goodbye' in English, which, he knew, was no news to me. However, he could have done what so many others do: they just ask you for some phrase in your language, try to repeat the exoticism and stay content with that.

on the screen and everyone can see who knows the anthem and who does not. How much fun one can have looking at those poor fellows getting confused over the lyrics and mumbling something, whatever it might be! To do them justice, not everyone is like that and there are plenty of footballers and lay people alike who have mastered their national anthem and would have no problem singing it if you woke them up in the middle of the night.

However, if you are one of those people who has had enough of Irish at school and has solemnly promised themselves to never have anything to do with this language again, there are other ways of expressing your Irishness. You won't have to speak Irish, but you will be doing VERY Irish things which sometimes have Irish names.

Everyone loves a good pint. What about a good pint in a cosy pub with a trad session in full swing? Traditional Irish music has long been a symbol of Irishness both locally and internationally. There are professional bands who play Irish music, but traditionally folk music happens when several locals come together with whatever instruments they can play and start a session. The instruments usually used to play traditional music are the fiddle, the uilleann pipes, the bodhrán, the flute, the tin whistle and the accordion, affectionately called the *bosca ceoil*, or 'music box' in Irish. Traditional music wouldn't be truly traditional if some of the instruments didn't have Irish names. *Bodhrán* is an Irish word for a special type of a drum (ironically, the same word is used to say 'a deaf person' – hardly a coincidence!) The uilleann pipes have managed to keep only a part of their original Irish name. They used to be known as *píobaí uilleann* which means 'pipes of the elbow': to play the pipes you have to squeeze the bellows with your elbow against your side. The half-translated term 'uilleann pipes' has been used since the beginning of the twentieth century. To split the never-ending upbeat rhythm created by this fine selection of instruments, a slow melancholic song is performed at many a session. It is sung in Irish and the style of singing is called *sean-nós*, which translates as 'the old way', i.e. old style. These songs usually tell stories of love, loss or Irish historical events.

Where there is music, there is dancing. Remember the céilís teenagers have in the Gaeltacht? If you had a whale of a time swinging in a community hall somewhere in Connemara, there is no need to give it up as you grow up and get that bank job in Dublin. There are céilí classes available for both beginners and more skilled dancers. Once you have brushed up on your steps, you can always take part in pub céilís or fundraising céilís.

Once a year traditional Irish music, singing and dancing come together in an ultimate celebration of Irish art – the all-Ireland festival *Fleadh Cheoil*, or 'the Music Festival'. It takes place in August and brings together the best musicians, singers and dancers who compete for the title of the best in each category. It's a spectacle not to be missed.

If you want something Irish and even more competitive than singing or dancing, then the GAA is heaven for you. The GAA, or the Gaelic Athletic Association, is an organisation which promotes traditional Irish sport. It was established in 1884 around the time when Ireland was beginning to revive its language and heritage in an attempt to claim back its nationhood and statehood. Taking part in old Irish games was meant to unite like-minded people and promote Irish culture in a popular way. If there was a prize for the most successful initiative to revive Irishness, the GAA would be the undisputed winner. The GAA has been hugely popular ever since its foundation. How big does it have to be if one of the former Taoisigh (Irish Prime Ministers), as well as ministers and other parliamentaries, prides himself on having played in the GAA and won medals?

Two main sports promoted by the GAA are Gaelic football and hurling. Not being a very sporty person, I would not be able to expain all the intricacies of these games but will give you a general idea. Gaelic football, in contrast to 'mainstream' football, i.e. soccer, is more relaxed about all the formalities like using hands and scoring goals. Do you feel like carrying the ball for a bit? Or fancy bouncing it on the ground before hand-passing it to your mate like in good old basketball? No problem at all, go for it. If you can't score a proper goal and the ball goes over the net, no need to worry, you are still a hero, just make sure it goes between the tall goal posts, and the point is yours! Hurling also involves a ball, points and goals but the ball is smaller and the players hit it with a stick. The aim of the game is to score a goal or a point by sending the ball flying between the goal posts. P.S. I promise to book my first Gaelic football ticket for this year's championship games and report back on all the details I left out here.

Although it is centered around sport, the GAA also promotes the Irish language and culture. According to the GAA rules and regulations, the players' names and surnames have to be written in Irish both on their jerseys and in the players' list for display. The team manager is called the *bainisteoir*. All the medals and trophies have to be inscribed in Irish. The equipment also has Irish names which are only sometimes used, but are definitely known to the team as well as eager supporters. The ball used in hurling, however, has developed a particular fondness for its Irish form, *sliotar*, which is commonly used on a par with the more prosaic 'hurling ball'. There is a whole booklet of useful terms and phrases in Irish which can be used before, during and after the game. The GAA always encourages its players to make as much use of Irish as possible.

There is a GAA club in literally every village. Then each county has its own passionately supported team which takes part in the All-Ireland championship every summer. The main GAA arena is Croke Park in Dublin. It is said to be the third largest stadium in Europe and it almost exclusively hosts GAA matches. The GAA is unique in that it is all about amateur sport. The players do not get paid for taking part in matches, even if they get as far as becoming all-Ireland champions. They have ordinary jobs. All the training and competing comes on top of their day-to-day duties. I used to have a colleague, a fellow English teacher, who was quite a star of the Dublin GAA team. Imagine the excitement of his students when they got a hands-on lesson in traditional Irish sport!

Tourist Tip

Feel like going 100 per cent Irish yourself? No problem at all. The Cobblestone, one of many Dublin pubs, is great for traditional music. If you are on your way to the Cliffs of Moher, pop into Ennis for a night. This town is like the capital of traditional music and singing. For the sports-inclined, Croke Park is a place to visit. The GAA has turned it into a tourist attraction with tours taking place daily. It received a Certificate of Excellence from TripAdvisor in 2015, so it is definitely worth checking out. Or even better, find out when the next GAA match is on, book your tickets and join hundreds of fans to do maybe the most Irish thing ever.

16 | SYSTEM UPGRADE

When it comes to surviving in the twenty-first century, Irish does not put all its eggs in the *sean-nós* basket. It adapts a new strategy and goes beyond purely Irish things, local and traditional. However popular and much loved these are by many, there are internationally minded people out there to be catered for. With new 'cool', global trends popping up here and there, Irish felt it could not afford to fall behind once again as it did in the nineteenth century: it went for a system upgrade.

It all started in 1972 when singer Sandy Jones was respresenting Ireland at the Eurovision song contest. She performed her song *'Ceol an Ghrá'* ('The Music of Love') in Irish. Sadly, the idea never took off and Irish has not made it to the Eurovision stage again since.

However, the Irish language did not give up and continued to use the media and entertainment as its main upgrading asset. In fact, the same year, 1972, an Irish language radio station, *Raidió na Gaeltachta*, was launched. As it did in its early days, it mainly serves the Gaeltacht communities, and, as a result, focuses on many issues of local interest. The presenters, for the most part, are native or extremely fluent speakers of Irish, often resorting to dialectal speech.

Although the launch of Raidió na Gaeltachta had been a major event for introducing Irish into the media domain, it soon became clear that traditional, local topics and a very high level of Irish typical of this radio station were a bit off-putting for young people or those who had less Irish. There was a need for a more engaging, urban and learner-oriented radio station. The void was filled by *Raidió na Life*. It is an independent radio station which was founded in 1993 in Dublin and took its name from the city's river Liffey. The simpler language the presenters speak, as well as a wider selection of topics, has made it very popular with Irish language learners. Following in the steps of Raidió na Life, a couple of online radio stations have popped up in recent years: *Raidió na dTreabh*, which serves Galway, and *Raidió Rí-Rá*, which makes Irish cool through music.

Another media power the Irish language embraced is television. An Irish language channel – *Teilifís na Gaeilge* – was first launched on state TV in 1996. It received its modern name, TG4 (pronounced *ti-gi-keahar*), in 1999. TG4 is one of the channels which form the basic TV package you get in Ireland. Nowadays TG4 tries to combine more traditional programmes about rural Ireland and local customs with Irish analogues of programmes which are popular all over the world.

Love the good old talk show? Join Máirtín Tom Sheáinín and his guests, who discuss a wide range of topics, mainly of Irish interest: from teaching prisoners how to build *naomhógs* (traditional Irish boats) to sharing memories about one's relatives who drowned on a much bigger boat, the *Titanic*.

If you are more of a *Strictly Come Dancing* fan, don't switch to BBC 1 – TG4 has something for you too. *Glór na Tíre* ('Voice of the Country') is a talent show for country and western performers. TG4 has broadcast other contests too which represent a clever mix of the traditional and the modern – the international genre of a talent show is applied to things that are Irish through and through. Isn't the very idea of a talent show for the best farmer adorable? Tune into *Feirm Factor*! Or vote for your favourite performer of traditional Irish music on *Gradaim Ceoil*.

Feel like something emotional? There is no shortage of drama in TG4's veteran show, the soap opera *Ros na Rún*. Set in a village in Connemara with colourful local characters, it contains all the plot twists we expect from a good soap. Is your finger hovering over that button to switch to ITV for an episode of *Blind Date*? No need – go for *Pioc Do Ride* ('Pick Your Ride') instead, and watch girls choose a guy based on his car – with all the choosing done through Irish!

Are there moody teenagers in your living room, sick of textbook Irish? *Aifric* is the answer. It is a teenage drama about a Dublin girl living in the West of Ireland – modern, topical but very local too. What else can you ask for? So thought the Irish film critics at the Irish Film and Television Academy too when they gave the series the IFTA Best Children's/Youth Programme award three years in a row (2007–2009). For the little Irish-speaking fans of *Harry Potter*, *Peppa the Pig* and *SpongeBob SquarePants*, TG4 went that extra mile and dubbed them into Irish. SpongeBob singing in Irish – now that *is* something, and freely available on YouTube to admire.

Don't get me wrong – SpongeBob songs *as Gaeilge* are amazing, but a bigger effort was needed to appeal to a somewhat pickier public: teenagers and young people. To win these guys over, Ed Sheeran had to step in. In 2015 he recorded his famous hit 'Thinking Out Loud' in Irish. Love Ed Sheeran? Get 'Ag Smaoineamh Ós Ard' with subtitles on YouTube and sing your favourite song in Irish. And Ed Sheeran is not alone. There is a new initiative to release an annual CD with famous songs resung by the same performers in Irish. Last year's *Ceol 2016* is now available online for downloading and includes Ed Sheeran's hit.

Dubbing works for books too, under the name of translation. You simply can't moan anymore that learning Irish is boring. Don't like reading the more traditional local stuff? Fair enough, what about *Harry Potter agus an Órchloch* (*Harry Potter and the Philosopher's Stone*) or *Cluiche na Corónach* (that is, *Game of Thrones*)? Irish rocks!

If you are a hardcore fan of *Game of Thrones*, I guess you will want that cool T-shirt saying *Game of Thrones: Winter is coming*. Well, Irish is already there, with a clever twist to the original slogan, turning fantasy into the comfort of good old eleven o'clock tea. The caption goes *Game of Scones: Tá bricfeasta ag teacht!* ('Game of Scones: Breakfast is coming') (see Picture 7).

Irish has confidently established itself in the field of T-shirt captions. There are several online shops where you can buy witty T-shirts with Irish phrases on them. Hairy Baby is a good one if you ask me. Otherwise, just pop into the Conradh na Gaeilge shop (*An Siopa Leabhar*) on Harcourt Street in Dublin where the products range from T-shirts with simple messages like *Labhair Gaeilge Liom Inniu* ('Speak Irish with me today') – a handy one if you are a learner and want more practice but are sometimes shy to ask for it – to more complex and often humorous captions.

What better way to finish off your Gaelic image than to wear your Irish language T-shirt to a yoga class *as Gaeilge*. And roll up your sleeves – so that everyone can admire that trendy Irish tattoo. No, I did not make that up – yoga and tattoos *as Gaeilge* do exist. Organ-ised yoga classes through Irish started in 2012 and have been run by an organisation called Óga Yoga ever since. Now you can even go on an Irish language yoga weekend to the Wicklow Mountains where you will meet like-minded people, relax, take in the scenery and practise your Irish. If you are still thinking of getting an Irish language tattoo before setting off on your yoga weekend, make sure you double-check what exactly those fancy Irish words mean. You do not want to be in the shoes of that poor guy whose unfortu-nate tattoo was all over the internet (as well as some national newspapers) recently. He got a lovely Celtic cross painted all over his back, with a ribbon running through the cross. To match the Celtic design of the cross, an Irish phrase on the ribbon was written in the old Gaelic script. What a fantastic piece of art for someone who is into all things Irish. But alas the solemnity of Irish tradition was mercilessly ruined by what the phrase actually said. Running proudly through the cross, it read '*An bhfuil cead agam dul go dtí an leithreas?*' Apparently, the man thought he was getting a tattoo saying 'You will forever be in my heart' (revise Chapter 14 if you are not laughing yet).[17]

It is highly unlikely that the tattoo story happened in Ireland or to an Irish person, as the *An bhfuil cead agam* bit of Irish never leaves the head of someone who has been through the Irish education system. However, make it one inch more challenging, and many will fall prey to the complexity of Irish. I have met people – solid

---

[17] If you want to admire the picture, you can see it in this article from the *Irish Independent*: http://www.independent.ie/entertainment/banter/trending/too-ridiculous-to-be-true-dodgy-tattoo-as-gaeilge-divides-internet-35365643.html.

supporters of Irish – who got really enthusiastic about such new uses of Irish as having their smartphone in Irish or using the Bank of Ireland ATM through Irish. They readily went for the Irish option but got so confused in the middle of it that one of them could not find the way to switch his phone back to English, while the ATM pioneer, when the machine asked him some extra questions before dispensing the money, had to quit the whole transaction and start all over again, this time sheepishly pressing the English language button.

17 | SURVIVAL CÚPLA FOCAL

Although Irish, let's face the truth, is not a widely spoken language throughout the country, it does have a strong presence in the life of the Irish population. Many people use what they call *cúpla focal* – a few words of Irish. Sometimes these are inserted at certain points in a conversation as a habit; in other cases they are the only names for certain phenomena. The latter is when the knowledge of Irish comes in handy for everyone who wants to spend time in Ireland, interacting with the locals.

If you are into politics, what's your opinion on how the Taoiseach addressed the TDs in the Dáil last night? Eh? Confused?

The Irish parliamentary system is based on the British model. However, its key elements reflect the ancient Gaelic order. The head of the government, called the Prime Minister in other countries, carries the name for a Gaelic chieftain – *An Taoiseach*. *Dáil* – a word which means a political or legal gathering or assembly – gave its name to the present-day parliament. As it is not strictly speaking the parliament, its members are not MPs – they are TDs, *teachtaí Dála*, members of the Dáil. Interestingly, the president of Ireland is called the President (with the Irish equivalent – *Uachtarán* – reserved for use in Irish only). However, the President does not live in his *residence*, he lives in *Áras an Uachtaráin*.

The tradition of giving Irish names to establishments of national importance goes beyond the political apparatus. If you want to travel around the country by bus, you will never find the main bus station on the map of Dublin. Look for *Bus Áras*. You can also take the *Luas* to *Bus Áras*. Never call it a tram. It is the Luas (*speed*).

Have you gotten lost or been robbed during your travels? Contact *An Garda Síochána* – the Guardians of Peace are always ready to help. *Gardaí* are really friendly and you can even take a picture with a *garda* (colloquially known as a *guard*) outside the General Post Office (see Picture 8).

An Post (never *the post!*) is another fascinating example of un-Britishising Ireland. World-famous red postboxes were once a part of the Irish landscape, with the monarch's initials imprinted on the side. However, after independence, something had to be done to them – they seemed far too British. Getting rid of them was impractical, so instead they were painted over in bright green, which also became the colour of every single *oifig an phoist* (post office). These old postboxes, silent witnesses to the tide of history, stand there now, still carrying famous royal initials like VR or GR,[18] tamed by emerald green. The Irish Free State of the 1920s also produced its own postboxes which carry the state's name in Irish, *Saorstát Éireann*. However, they are scarce, as the Free State was renamed Ireland in 1937 and later the Republic of Ireland. Newly manufactured postboxes carried *P&T* (Posts and Telegraphs) written in the old Gaelic script. (See Picture 9.)

---

[18] VR stands for Victoria Regina (Queen Victoria) and GR for George Rex (King George V).

Stamps produced by An Post inevitably say *Éire* rather than Ireland, sending the message of the Irish identity to the whole world. 2015 Christmas stamps greeted the world with the word *Nollaig,* which is Irish for Christmas (see Picture 10). Each electricity bill, which An Post delivers, gives you an option *do bhille a fháil i nGaeilge* – to receive it in Irish, in other words.

Bus, train and Luas stops are announced in two languages; bus and coach destinations at the front of a vehicle change from English to Irish and back.

Private businesses do not fall behind. Some shops choose to display certain information on their fronts in Irish. For example, Irish might be used to say what kind of shop it is, what products or services it offers, what its opening hours are, and whether it is open or closed at the moment (see Picture 11). Such use of the Irish language on shop fronts is more common in or near the Gaeltachts though, for example in Galway city. The use of Irish in your business name or advert usually conveys the messages of localness, quality and tradition.

The whole town of Clonakilty in the southwest of Ireland made bilingual shop fronts a basis for its new image. The idea was to turn Clonakilty from a shabby backwater town into a holiday resort. New cafés were opened and shopfronts repainted, but it was the Irish language that added the final touch of localness and tradition. Clonakilty is also famous for its meat produce which is sold throughout the country. To emphasise its quality, both Clonakilty sausages and Clonakilty black pudding have the Irish equivalents of their English names on the package (see Picture 12).

In the age of globalisation some international brands have decided to signal that they value the area where they are based, that they are a local version of the brand, catering for the local population. Nothing comes in as handy in this situation as a sprinkle of Irish. The British supermarket chain Tesco, which is well-established in Ireland, has *Fáilte* and *Slán* signs ('Welcome' and 'Goodbye') as well as bilingual sign-posting inside the store (see Picture 13). A world-famous coffee chain, Costa, feels the need to cater for Galwegians by welcoming them to Costa Galway city in Irish: *Fáilte roimh Costa Coffee Cathair na Gaillimhe* is neatly written on the wall inside the café. Even McDonalds goes out of its way and suggests that you share your fantastic Coke with your *dearthair* (that is, brother) after you have eaten your *McMór* (no Big Macs here, we can do it in Irish!) (see Picture 14).

Culture Pool

Crack (to give its English spelling) is a quintes-sentially Irish concept – having a good time with your friends, usually in a pub. The word is often assumed to have come from Irish. However, the real story is more complicated. It had originally been an English word which was borrowed by the Irish language in the mid-twentieth century with the gaelicised spelling '*craic*'. Since the concept of a good time in good company was so dear to the Irish soul, the word for it thrived in Irish, was then reborrowed by English and has ever since been associated with Ireland and the type of English spoken by Irish people. 'What's the craic?' they might ask you. It is just a local way of saying 'how are you, any news?' OK, enough linguistics, go to The Gingerman – a lovely pub next to Trinity College – and have your bit of craic. P.S. Look out for the Irish language decor upstairs!

Many pubs throughout the country will have the phrases *Bia agus Deoch, Ceol agus Craic* on their fronts. No need to panic. They promise the simple pleasures of food, drink, music and, well, craic (see Picture 15). Pubs with their *craic*-promising signs set an example for some more serious public bodies. There is a definite tendency for especially socially focused organisa-tions and charities to take up Irish names. They look unusual, concise and patriotic. *Abhaile* instead of 'a mortgage debt consultancy', *An Taisce* instead of 'the Irish heritage trust', *Madra* instead of 'a dog rescue' or *Team Obair* instead of 'recruitment services'. However, at the bottom of it all, these names are a mere symbolic nod to the Irish language. If you decided to translate them into English, all you will get is a mortgage debt consultancy called *Home*, the Irish Heritage Trust *Treasure*, a dog rescue service called *Dog* and recruit-ment services *Team Work*. I am not sure that the same kind of simple names would have been given to these organisations had they opted for an English name. It is a nice nod to the Irish language no doubt but these translations highlight the tendency of keeping a safe distance from Irish as a fully functional language and sticking to the comfortably simple *cúpla focal* which are sure not to confuse or upset anyone.

From public organisations and shop fronts, the *cúpla focal* have also made their way into people's speech. They are a limited number of words or phrases used in limited contexts. For example, if you want to say that you speak a little bit of Irish, you will say, 'yes, I have *cúpla focal Gaeilge*'. *Cúpla focal* is used to refer to the knowledge of any language. If someone is going to Spain, you can say, 'yes, he knows *cúpla focal* Spanish'. *Gaeilge*, the name of the language, is often used instead of 'Irish', so you speak *as Gaeilge* rather than 'in Irish'. A response to the news of someone's death is often expressed through Irish: *Ar dheis Dé go raibh a anam*, 'may his soul be at the right hand of God'. People can say it instead of 'RIP'; it is also a common feature of newspaper death notices and actual gravestones throughout the country.

Individual Irish words also pop up here and there in everyday speech. Sometimes the word 'generous' is substituted with a pseudo-Irish *flaithulach*. I say 'pseudo' because it looks genuine, with a typical Irish adjective ending, *–ach*, but the original word for 'generous' is actually *flaithiúil*. Saying *fáilte* and *slán* for 'welcome' and 'goodbye' are quite common if people want to emphasise their Irishness or know that both they and the person they are talking to share an interest in the Irish language. When drinking, Irish people tend to say 'cheers' in Irish: *sláinte*. Another word most Irish people remember from school, if not from crèche, is *geansaí* (sweater), an important word indeed in this windy country. The Luas advertising team decided to trigger people's childhood memories and include *geansaí* in their 2016 Christmas ad. To celebrate the beginning of Christmas season people were encouraged to wear their *gensaí Nollag* on a certain day and get a free Luas ride (see Picture 16). You need your *cúpla focal* after all, don't you?

Other uses of Irish in speech are more person-dependent. For example, in my in-laws' family, water is referred to as *uisce* and we are often invited to come in and sit down through Irish. The 'Our Father' before lunch can also turn into *Ár n-Athair*. If someone is in the mood, they can insert a random Irish word they know instead of the English one. In my experience, *cúpla focal* are usually used in a light-hearted conversation when people are in a jolly mood or are being a little bit cheeky. My friends, for example, went for a *sos beag* rather than 'a quick break' at a recent pub quiz.

Finally, I have noticed a tendency to use Irish words as euphemisms. I have heard *leithreas* used instead of 'toilet' and *ospidéal* instead of 'hospital'.

Irish All Around You | 18

Even if you miss these sprinkles of Irish in speech or the media, do not worry. You can't possibly miss the encounter with this language altogether. Look at any road sign – it's there, leaping out at you. Or walk down Grafton Street around Christmas – *Nollaig Shona Duit*, say the illuminated letters (see Picture 17). Happy Christmas!

Irish has not always been a feature of local signage. Only after independence had been gained did the state start recovering Irish versions of placenames and reintroducing them into the so-called linguistic landscape (signage) of the country. As late as 2003, the *Official Languages Act* made Irish compulsory on all state signs, which include street and placenames, government buildings, state-funded organisations and public transport. Irish comes before English on these types of signs. In compliance with official regulations, the letter size is identical for both languages. The Irish version, however, is often given in italics, so that the two inscriptions do not flow one into the other. As for the Gaeltacht, the *Official Languages Act* prescribes that all the signs be solely in Irish. This change has not been welcomed by everyone. People complain that it makes reading the road signs slow, especially for non-locals. Tourism is also an issue: tourists may never recognise their old favourite spot behind a new, long and confusing Irish name.

The most famous debate on Irish placenames centred around a touristy town in the Kerry Gaeltacht in the southwest of the country. It has always been known as Dingle but, as a result of the 2003 *Languges Act*, had to appear on all signs exclusively in its Irish form, *An Daingean*. The locals were concerned, not only over the disappearence of the English version, but also because there was another town in Ireland known as *An Daingean* in Irish. The conflict took six years (2005–2011) to resolve. A residents' referendum had to be organised. In the end, Dingle retained its English form alongside a rather more complicated Irish one: it is now officially *Dingle* or *Daingean Uí Chúis* – they wanted to be clear of any association with the other Daingean, after all! Never mind the name though; go and visit good old Dingle, enjoy its pubs and make friends with the local celebrity, Fungie the friendly dolphin.

The confusion on the part of tourists, which Dingle locals were afraid of, sends us back in history to the time when places got their names. Why indeed are they so different in English and in Irish? And are they always different?

It is a very long and complicated story; in fact, so long and complicated that a separate field of research on Irish placenames has emerged. Here we will talk only about the basics.

There are different stories behind different places. The majority of them originally bore an Irish name. When the British government commissioned the Ordnance Survey of Ireland in the nineteenth century, all the geographical names had to be written down onto a map. Irish words did not make much sense to British surveyers, so they spelt the placenames the English way, just as they heard them, without bothering too much about the Irish original. Usually meaningful and poetic Irish names were turned into often strange and meaningless combination of letters. There is a lovely train stop outside Dublin called *Glenageary* – one of those numerous names which do not really mean anything, you might say with a shrug (see Picture 18). Well, read the Irish version underneath: *Gleann na gCaorach*, the valley of the sheep. So Irish! Or take Dublin's (and one of Europe's) biggest city park – the Phoenix Park. A slightly unrealistic but nice name, you might think. Sure why not, maybe phoenixes existed after all. No they didn't, a strict Irish scholar will say. The original Irish name of the area is connected with mineral springs which have been running through the park since ancient times. *Fionn Uisce* – clear water – was what people called it, but to an English ear it sounded more like 'phoenix', so it became the *Phoenix Park* in English while remaining *Páirc an Fhionnuisce* in Irish.

Meaning is no joke. One can eventually grow suspicious of the peaceful character of this island when passing through places like Kilmacanogue, Kilmainham, Shankill, Kildare, and finally, simply, Kill. So agressive! Or is it? Not at all, in fact. *Cill* is an old Irish word for a church. It is no surprise that Ireland, the land of early Christian missionaries, had churches all over the island. The Church of St Mocheanóg, the Church of the Monks, Old Church, the Church of the Oak and simply the Church – this is what these place-names meant originally.

In other cases, surveyers must have been more inquisitive about the meaning of the original Irish name because there are places whose English name is a direct translation from Irish. There is a wonderfully named place in Connemara, in the West – a group of islands in a lake known as *Oileáin Fataí*. The English name is a direct translation from Irish – Potato Islands.

Sometimes, however, well-meaning surveyors got confused, which, many people think, was the case with the village of Roundstone in Connemara. Its Irish name is *Cloch na Rón*, the stone of the seal, not a round stone, however similar *rón* and *round* might sound to an English ear.

Other places with word-for-word translations are young and modern, so they have never had an Irish name. The English one is their original name whereas the Irish one was given to them later as a translation from English. For example, Greystones, a seaside town once frequented by the Anglo-Irish aristocracy, had been established as Greystones in 1855. Later on, after independence, an Irish form was created: *Na Clocha Liatha*, Grey Stones.

These retrospective translations can sometimes go too far. There is a road in Dublin called Stoney Road. Eager translators quickly baptised it *Bóthar na gCloch*. A stony road indeed! However, the road had in fact originally been named after physicist George Johnstone Stoney (1826–1911), so it is very unlikely that there had been any Irish stony-stony road behind it. The mistranslation has recently been detected, so new shiny *Bóthar Stoney* signs have been put up in place of the old *Bóthar na gCloch* ones. But the locals well remember the times just a few years ago when the road was still *stone-y* for Irish speakers.

In some cases several Irish versions of a placename co-exist, although only one is chosen to be official and to appear on the national placenames database.[19]

---

[19] The database is available online at www.logainm.ie.

For example, in a Dublin suburb of Dundrum, there is a little road called Taney Rise. It is just under 500 metres long but contains two competing street name plaques. The older one translates Taney Rise as *Ard Tí Naithí*, that is 'the rise of the house of Naithí' (a male name). 'House' in this context usually means 'a house of a saint', that is, a church. And there is a church there all right. And everything would have been fine if not for another sign, a new shiny one, just fifty metres up the road. The newcomer wants to make life simpler – forget the house of Naithí, it is all history long gone and forgotten, let's be modern and try not to overcomplicate our lives. Let's make it simply *Ard Taney* (see Picture 19).

Certain placenames are completely different in Irish and in English. Do you think you will get anywhere nice if you follow the sign for *Baile Átha Cliath?* Sounds long and backwaterish? Well, it is no more, no less than Dublin, the capital. Why so different? Actually, both names are of Irish origin. As we learned earlier, Dublin was founded by the Vikings. Their settlement was known in Irish as 'Black Pool' – *Dubh Linn.* However, further up the river, there was a local Celtic settlement called 'Town of the Hurdled Ford' – *Baile Átha Cliath* in Irish.

Whereas most placenames outside the Gaeltacht hold an Irish and an English name, there are a couple of bold ones which, as if to take revenge after independence, got rid of their English names altogether. The boomerang effect, psychologists would say.

There is a lovely harbour in south Dublin. Indeed, it is so pleasant that back in 1821 King George IV ordered a port to be built there to replace the older village. After the king's visit to the newly constructed port, the place was named Kingstown. One hundred years later, in the newly born independent Ireland, there was little reverance for the British monarchy, and Kingstown had to change its name. Who wants to drop a royal title though? Luckily, Kingstown did not have to do it; all that was needed was a switch of affiliations: from the British to the old Irish monarchy. Before 1821, when there was no port, there was a village by the harbour. It formed around an old fort which was built in the late fifth century by the then High King of Ireland, Lóegaire (or Laoghaire). So when the 1920s came, all Kingstown had to do was to go back to its roots and re-adopt its original name, *Dún Laoghaire* – the fort of King Laoghaire. This has been its official name in both languages since then.

A similar trick was performed with one of the midland Irish counties. The land was occupied by the English in 1548 and eight years later Queen Mary modestly named it Queen's County. The independent state of the 1920s swiftly rectified this historical injustice and gave the county its original Irish name *Laois*, which comes from the medieval Irish kingdom of Loígis.

However fascinating the history of Irish placenames is, it might seem to some people a bit too local and of little relevance for the rest of the world. Wait till I prove them wrong. If you have a car and are a nature lover, you are more than likely to go on a day trip to Dublin's neighbouring County Wicklow. Driving along the windy moutain roads, sooner or later you will see a sign for Hollywood. What? Is it a joke or a local delusion of grandeur? Neither.

The village of Hollywood is an ancient and sacred place where fascination with nature and Irish ancient Christian tradition come together. Holly, a red-berried bush, is pretty widespread in the area, so that it came to be known as *Cnoic Rua* in Irish, that is 'the Red Hill', or, to put it in more prosaic English, 'the Wood of Holly

Bushes', Hollywood for short. However, as with every self-respecting hollywood, the Irish hollywood was not just a hill with vegetation on it but a highly popular place too. The 'Red Hill' was made famous by an Irish saint, St Kevin, who lived in the sixth century. St Kevin, looking for a tranquil place to settle and devote himself to prayer, passed through Hollywood and walked as far as a beautiful valley with two lakes, which is known as Glendalough. He settled there and founded a monastery which soon became a well-known religious site. St Kevin, known to be a man of great holiness in his lifetime, continues to be much venerated by Christians to this day. Devotion to St Kevin brought a flow of pilgrims to Glendalough. They all wanted to follow in St Kevin's footsteps as they were travelling to the monastery, so they all passed through Hollywood, now made *Holy Wood* by St Kevin and his flock (however, it is spelled 'Hollywood', nicely preserving both identities of the place). The Irish name for Hollywood used nowadays also reflects a connection with St Kevin. It associates the place with a church which must have been built in Hollywood around or after St Kevin's time, in the thirteenth century at the latest.[20] It is endearingly called 'the Churchlet of St Kevin', *Cillín Chaoimhín*.

There was a man in Hollywood/Cillín Chaoimhín called Matthew Guirke. He lived during the Great Famine in the mid-nineteenth century. When he was

---

[20] The original church is now gone. It is difficult to pinpoint its location but it is believed that it might have stood on the site of the current Church of Ireland church, which was built there in the seventeenth century. Source: 'Medieval Pilgrimage at Hollywood, County Wicklow', *Pilgrimage in Medieval Ireland*, https:// pilgrimagemedievalireland.com/2012/09/05/medieval-pilgrimage-at-hollywood-co-wicklow/.

in his twenties, his family, unable to feed themselves through farming, decided to emigrate to America. Matthew settled in California and with time earned enough money to buy a race track. Money did not go to his head through, and he never forgot his humble native village. Matthew named the race track Hollywood. The name later spread to the area around it, so that when the first film-makers arrived to establish their studios there, they were already dealing with Hollywood. All they had to do was to make it famous.

Ironically, the original Hollywood has recently become a true Irish Hollywood because quite a few films, including those produced by Hollywood, were filmed in Hollywood. Oops. Did you get it? Basically, the scenery in and around the village of Hollywood in Ireland is so beautiful that it attracted local as well as American film-makers. Watch *King Arthur* (the old one), *Braveheart*, *Dancing at Lughnasa* or indeed *P.S. I Love You* and experience Hollywood (pun!) at its best.

Culture Pool

Although we ended the story of Irish placenames on a light note, do not forget that all the fun of comparing Irish and English names comes from the notorious renaming campaign of the nineteenth century. There is a whole play about it: *Translations* by Brian Friel. It is an insightful depiction of history being remade and identities shifting when a foreign language with a new way of thinking is being forced on a nation. The linguistic scars from that time are still there, staring at us from every bilingual road sign, reminding us of the troubled history of Ireland, its people and its language.

Picture 1

Picture 2

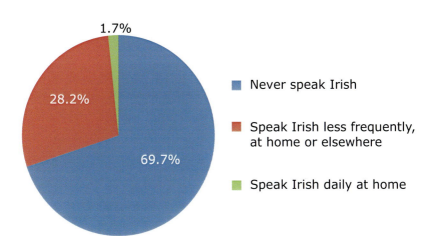

1.7%

28.2%

69.7%

■ Never speak Irish

■ Speak Irish less frequently,
at home or elsewhere

■ Speak Irish daily at home

* This chart excludes 0.3% of people who did not state how
often they spoke Irish

Picture 3

Picture 4: Map © Údarás na Gaeltachta. Reproduced with permission. Gaeltacht areas are marked in dark green.

Picture 5: Map © Údarás na Gaeltachta. Reproduced with permission. The Great Blasket is circled in black and the Aran Islands in red.

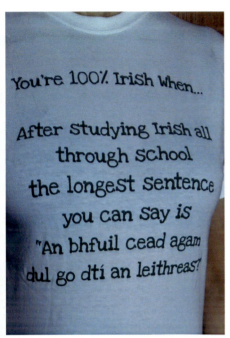

You're 100% Irish when...

After studying Irish all
through school
the longest sentence
you can say *is*
"An bhfuil cead agam
dul go dtí an leithreas?"

Picture 6

GAME OF SCONES

TÁ BRICFEASTA
AG TEACHT

Picture 7

GARDA

Picture 8

Picture 9

Picture 10

Picture 11

Picture 12

Picture 13

Picture 14

Picture 15

Picture 16

Picture 17

Picture 19

Picture 18

PART II

IRISH: A BIT OF LINGUISTICS (ARE IRISH AND ENGLISH VERY SIMILAR LANGUAGES)?

Me: I am trying to learn some Irish in my free time.
My curious friend: Oh yes, and is it very different from English? It must be easy for you; your English is fluent.
Me: ------------------ *(mentally rolling on the floor in linguistic convulsions)*
My curious friend: REALLY?

My dotted answer, as you might have guessed, is a big definitive *no*. But is it really enough to know the right answer without understanding the reasons? I hope you will be a model reader and answer *'Of course not!'*, otherwise I might as well throw the rest of this section into the bin.

There are two ways of illustrating that Irish and English are very different languages – a fun way and an academic way. We may as well start with some anecdotes to get us going and then offer our brain something more challenging.

19 | WHICH IS THE RIGHT BATHROOM?

When I started my minor in Celtic Studies, one of my lecturers, trying to give the students a break from the complexities of Celtic linguistics, told us this anecdote. I am afraid I do not remember when exactly the story took place. Nor whether it was a true story or simply a joke passed on from one Celtic scholar to another – most likely it was a combination of both. This does not change the essence of the anecdote though.

A foreign academic was travelling to Dublin. He had quite a background in classical and modern languages but had no word of Irish. He was not overly worried about this (and you can probably see why, having read the first part of the book). But it is always dangerous to travel to a country without having a clue about its language. Upon the professor's arrival in Dublin airport, as he was passing through all the turmoil of checks and customs and luggage belts, he needed a bathroom. Alas, *Gents* and *Ladies* were written in Irish only and there were no pictures on the doors either. He had a choice between *Fir* and *Mná*. Surely this linguistic puzzle should not intimidate a learned man? In the major European languages he spoke, the two sexes were described through similar words derived from the well-known Latin *masculīnus* and *fēminīnus*. *Male* and *female* in English, *Männer* and *Frauen* in German, *masculin* and *féminin* in French, *masculino* and *feminino* in Spanish.[21] They all look a little bit different, but the root and the meaning are unmistakably the same. Pleased to have solved the Irish puzzle, our professor proudly marched through the 'Mná' door – only to find that Irish is so different from the mainstream European languages, including English, that *Fir* stands for 'men' and *Mná* for 'women'!

However entertaining the anecdote may be, I have to tell you that it is unlikely that an Irish-only sign without any accompanying pictures was ever displayed at an international airport. Even if the story is 100 percent true, the bathrooms at Dublin airport are not that dangerous anymore. At the same time, Irish on bathroom signs throughout the country is not rare. It is usually accompanied either by English or a picture, or both. However, I have spotted one of those vicious *Fir* and *Mná* toilets in St Enda's Park in Dublin, as recently as 8 May 2017. Beware! (See Picture 20.)

If our professor, deeply embarrassed by his linguistic mistake, were ever to look into why Irish is so different from English, he would turn to the knowledge of historians and linguists.

---

[21] There are also alternative adjectives available for 'feminine' in German (*weiblich*) and 'masculine' in French and Spanish (*homme* and *hombre* respectively).

20 | HOW A HISTORIAN SEES IT

It is easy to assume that if two languages are spoken on neighbouring territories or coexist within one territory they are similar, or, in linguistic terms, closely related. Indeed, such examples are numerous. Take Swedes, Danes and Norwegians, whose countries are neighbours. Their languages, known as Scandinavian, are similar to an extent that a speaker of one of them is able to read in the other two, and even have a conversation if both parties are patient and willing to accommodate. Indeed, it is possible for similar languages to be spoken on neighbouring territories if these territories have been populated by ethnically close groups of people, and no major population movements or conquests of land have taken place.

However, as we all know, it had been common for whole ethnicities to move around the Eurasian continent before modern European nations started to form around the seventeenth and eighteenth centuries. As a result, some ethnicities found themselves surrounded by genetically and linguistically unrelated peoples. For example, Swedes and Norwegians, two 'cousin' nations, share the Scandinavian Peninsula with Finns, who are historically so different that they are more like an old friend than a relative to the other two. And yet, two separate population movements brought them together.

Similarly, the English and the Irish had originally been two ethnically different groups which did not share the same territory, and spoke linguistically distant languages. However, in the course of history, they came into contact with each other, producing the modern Irish nation and causing the long-term coexistence of the Irish and English languages.

Anglo-Saxons, speakers of what was to become the English language, were Germanic tribes who originally lived on the continent, on the northwest coast of modern Germany, the Netherlands and Denmark. They migrated to Britain in the fifth century AD to find earlier inhabitants who were of a different ethnicity and spoke a very different language. These were Celts. They had come to Britain and Ireland as early as around 500 BC from southern Europe (Italy and Spain) and spoke Celtic languages which later evolved into modern Irish, Welsh and Scottish Gaelic, not forgetting Cornish and Manx. With time, the balance tipped towards the newcomers. Anglo-Saxons suppressed the Celtic peoples in Britain and then conquered the ones in Ireland, but the two distinct ethnicities and languages have continued to coexist both in Ireland and in Britain to this day.

21 | HOW A LINGUIST SEES IT

Linguists are usually pretty good at history and try to incorporate it in their studies. What if they weren't? Would they be able to establish which languages are closely related and which have barely any connection with each other through pure language analysis? No doubt they could, and I will show you how.

Most languages go very far back in time to their ancestors, called proto-languages. Many thousands of years ago there was a limited number of these proto-languages. As time went by and the human population of the earth grew and spread over new territories, each proto-language gradually dissolved into a bunch of separate languages. Scared and confused, the newly born languages stuck to their groups and formed language families, each cherishing the memory of their patriarch.

The family we are interested in is the powerful Indo-European family, which now consists of 437 living languages.[22] In each family, there are members for whom ancestral traditions are hugely important. These members are proud of being a typical representative of the clan. There are also members who are more individualistic and want to find their own way in this world. They wander astray and end up leading lives very different from the rest of the family. There are cousins who are best friends and love all the same

---

[22] Data taken from *Ethnologue: Languages of the World* (www.ethnologue.com).

83

things; and there are cousins who avoid family occasions just so that they don't bump into each other. The Indo-European language family is no exception here. There are members who stick together, look similar and work in a similar way. They form groups: Germanic languages, Romance languages, Celtic languages – have a look at the family tree in Picture 21. You might have guessed now, as you are studying the tree, that English and Irish are not that close at all. Distant cousins forced to share a house but leading two very separate lives. There are members devoted to the ways of their ancestors – like Lithuanian or German – who have preserved as best they could the complex grammatical structure and much of the original vocabulary. There are also black sheep of the family like Irish and its Celtic cousins. They were very bold when they were young, so they went off and got rid of many of their ancestral features in favour of some exotic gifts a mysterious stranger once offered them. The stranger was soon gone, but the cousins were destined to bear the gifts until the end of times, wrecking the heads of many good people ever since.

To be more specific and more academic, the essential grammar and vocabulary, which are usually shared by Indo-European languages, show clear signs of difference in the case of the Celtic cousins. It has been speculated that when Celtic tribes arrived in Ireland and Britain they came into contact with an earlier, unknown non-Indo-European population of the islands. The Celts must have conquered them and 'devoured' them together with their language, keeping some of the linguistic features in their own Celtic languages. Who those tribes were and which languages they spoke is a mystery which historians and linguists have been struggling to solve for over half a century. Afro-Asiatic, Basque and Altaic languages are mentioned by different scholars. Foreign influences and early isolation from most of the other Indo-European languages, as well as natural language development, have left Irish some very peculiar features which a speaker of an average European language[23] wouldn't dream of (except for a nightmare perhaps). Be they daunting or fascinating, just flip over to the next chapter, and here they are – the features of the Irish language which will not leave your linguistic heart untouched.

---

[23] In the sense of European languages of the Indo-European family.

APPEARANCES ARE OFTEN DECEPTIVE | 22

Despite what the wise old proverb says, we all tend to base our first impressions of someone or something on their appearance. So we might as well start our excursion into the curiosities of Irish by learning about its physical form, because the appearance of Irish can be very deceptive indeed, to such an extent that you would have no idea that the random notches you are looking at are actually the Irish language. Compare, for example, the three images in Picture 22. The phrase 'son of Ciarán' represents the development of the Irish writing system from the fourth century until the present day. Version 1 is the earliest form of Irish writing (the fourth to seventh centuries AD), version 2 illustrates the script used between the seventh and the mid-twentieth centuries, while version 3 is present-day written Irish.[24]

The Irish have not always been using the Latin alphabet to write down their language. First, they had their own alphabet called *Ogham*. It consisted of 20 main letters which were represented by longer lines (pointing right, left or across) and shorter, sometimes dot-like straight lines. The longer lines were used for consonants (*m, c, t,* etc.) whereas the shorter sometimes dot-like ones were reserved for vowels (*a, o, e,* etc.) – you can see how it all worked in practice on

---

[24] The phrase 'son of Ciarán' was chosen because it is a part of an Ogham inscription on a stone in Corrower, Gallen, Co. Mayo (stone ID CIIC).

the Ogham stone shown in Picture 23. The majority of inscriptions appear on standing stones and should be read from the bottom of the stone all the way up the left side, and then down the right side. The boom of Ogham writing was in the fifth and sixth centuries AD. Most surviving Ogham stones are in the southwest of Ireland, with a fine collection of them a couple of miles from the town of Dingle.

Just imagine, a brownish gloomy hill on the horizon or a lush green field stretching as far as the eye can see, and a lone standing stone covered in mysterious inscriptions of old. What messages did the carvers leave? I bet you are thinking that those stones, proudly standing against the stunning Irish landscape, carry some deeply magical words. In that case, you are in for a disappointment. Things are very prosaic indeed. The stones carry people's names, usually in the form of 'someone, son of someone'. The stones are thought to have been used to commemorate people (just as is done nowadays) or to mark territory.

With the advent of the seventh century, and as Christianity confidently established itself in Ireland, the Latin alphabet started to take over and the first handwritten books appeared: who would be carving stones if you could now be flying all over the page with a quill pen? Handwriting became art, and Irish scriptors did their best to give Latin letters that unique Celtic twist. When the first book in Irish was printed in 1571, handwritten samples were used, so the Latin letters were printed with the same Celtic twist, known nowadays as the *Gaelic type* or the *(Old) Gaelic script*.

However, as time went by and books started to be mass produced, a less elaborate, more down-to-earth, standard and, dare I say, international font seemed to be more appropriate. The Gaelic type was taken out of use in the mid-twentieth century, so contemporary printed Irish looks very much like contemporary printed English (or French or Italian for that matter).

Not quite, though. The Irish language does not use all the letters of the Latin alphabet. You won't find any *j, k, q, v, w, x, y* or *z* in Irish words (except for such black sheep as *zú* ('zoo')). Also, Irish uses an accent sign above vowels (like this: *á*) to show that the vowel is long. The Irish word for the accent sign is the *fada*, which means 'long'.

The Gaelic type is not *gone* gone though. It is still used in Irish (and not only in Irish, as you will find out in Chapter 38) for decorative purposes. You might see a pub somewhere in Dingle or Connemara whose name is written in Irish (one point for authenticity) and in the old script (that extra authentic quality to attract one more busload of visitors). The old script is not all fun for tourists though. It can also be a sign of solemnity, respect and deep affection. Some of the gravestones in Irish-speaking regions carry inscriptions in Irish, and the old script is not a rarity there. The same goes for monuments commemorating national heroes or events of particular importance, for example, a poem on the wall of the Garden of Remembrance in Dublin, commemorating all those who fought for Irish freedom over the centuries (see Picture 24).

23 | IN LOVE WITH THE VERB

If you ever arm yourself with a dictionary and attempt to decode that Gaelic-type inscription on the Garden of Remembrance wall, you will find a really weird thing. *Chuireamar ár n-aisling ag snámh mar eala ar an abhainn,* /***Rinneadh*** *fírinne den aisling* (literally '**Sent** we our dream swimming like swans on the river,/**Came** our dream true').[25] Have you spotted it? Every positive sentence starts with the verb. No need to panic, we are all a bit different. Most European languages start a sentence with the subject (a person or a thing) whereas the Irish language decided that actions speak louder than words and put the verb in the initial position. Well, we have to learn to accept each other's differences and, in the case of Irish, get used to constantly saying things like 'Study I Irish and read I books every day.' That's just the way it is. These were just standard positive sentences, note you. Wait till you see what is going on in the questions and answers department.

Yes and *No, Ja* and *Nein, Oui* and *Non, Tak* and *Nie* are natural and straightforward answers which fly off our lips without much effort. Well, as long as we do not attempt to speak Irish. Here is what the Irish 'yes' answers look like:

Are you all right? – ***Tá.***
Are you a student? – ***Is ea.***
Do you go there often? – ***Téim.***

---

[25] The poem was written by Liam Mac Uistín in 1976 and is called 'An Aisling' in Irish and 'We Saw a Vision' in English.

*Did you read yesterday? – **Léigh.***
*Will you come again? – **Tiocfaidh.***
Impressive, isn't it?
The 'No' answers at least have the decency to always start the first word with 'n':
*Are you all right? – **Níl.***
*Are you a student? – **Ní hea.***
*Do you go there often? – **Ní théim.***
*Did you read yesterday? – **Níor léigh.***
*Will you come again? – **Ní thiocfaidh.***
The idea behind those mad answers is that it is the verb from the question that is used as the answer. To give a positive answer, we just repeat the verb used in the question (*Do you love me? – Love*); the negative answer is that verb with a corresponding 'no' particle (*Do you love me? – Don't love*).

24 | AS CHANGEABLE AS THE WEATHER

What do languages like English, German, French or Russian do if they need to signal the gender of a noun, put the verb into the past tense, or do other things like that? Of course they use special endings. For example, the English *clean* becomes *clean**ed*** in the past tense, or the French adjective *bon* becomes *bon**ne*** if it is followed by a feminine noun. But Irish has its own way. Why bother with endings? Simply mutate the words themselves, no need to fuss over them!

Basically, in certain situations, the first sound of the word changes, which is reflected in spelling by adding 'h' after the letter in question or putting an extra letter at the beginning of a word. For example: *ceannagh – **ch**ennaigh* ('buy' – 'bought') or *bus – ar an **m**bus* ('bus' – 'on the bus').

The rules of how and when words mutate are all over Irish grammar. Mutations are quite powerful as they can signal a change of gender, number, case or tense. Just to give you a flavour of these mutations, here are some examples:

A cara – her friend

*A **ch**ara* – his friend

*A **g**cara* – their friend

Imagine trying to prove that it is HIS fault but, overpowered by emotion, you lose control for a split second and let that one fatal slip of the tongue happen, and suddenly it is someone else's fault. Those mutations could have easily sent a couple of innocent people to the gallows in the old times (I sincerely hope they did not though).

SO YOU THINK ENGLISH PRONUNCIATION IS TOUGH? | 25

Irish pronunciation is very confusing, and mutations are one of the reasons. You need to remember how to pronounce them: which sound turns into which and how this is reflected in writing. Also do not forget that a consonant can undergo two mutations and thus exists in three forms: original, lenited (softened) and nasalised. For example, the quite innocent *b* turns into the lenited *bh* (pronounced 'v'), and nasalised *mb* (pronounced 'm'). For example, you make *an botún* (mistake), then you realise the foolishness of *an bhotúin* you have just made but, thankfully, you soon 'do forgetting', as we say in Irish, *ar an mbotún*.[26]

At the end of the day, mutated consonants are not that bad: there are at least fixed rules for pronouncing them. In many other cases half the letters in a word are not pronounced, while the other half are pronounced in a completely unexpected way, and there are rarely any rules to help. How is a young gullible learner of Irish expected to know that the evil 'f' in the word *féin* (self) is often pronounced 'h'?

Time for a challenge. Read it out loud: *bhfaighidh* ('I will get').

Tried? Failed? Partially? It's understandable. *Bhf* (which is a mutated *f*), is pronounced 'w', the rest boils

---

[26] To explain it in more academic terms, the masculine noun *botún* ('mistake') changes *b* to *bh* after the article in the genitive case and adds *m* at the beginning of the word after a preposition plus the article.

down to 'aihi': uncomfortable-looking *gh* and *dh* are silently ignored. The answer is **'waihi'**. Simply **'waihi'**.[27]

---

[27] Pronunciation may differ from dialect to dialect. The form given here is likely to be heard in the Connacht dialect (Galway and Mayo).

THE MAGNIFICENT ELEVEN | 26

If you have ever tried to learn or teach a European language like English, German, French or Spanish, you will find the term 'irregular verbs' quite familiar. There is a chance that you will also remember tables and lists of those cheeky verbs which do not obey the regular pattern when they are used in the past or the perfect form. Let me give you an example from English. The general rule is to add *-ed* or *-d* to the initial form of the verb in order to form a past or a perfect tense form: *jump–jumped–have jumped*. And then come the irregulars: *drive–drove–driven*, *go–went–gone*, *think–thought–thought*, *build–built–built* and even *put–put–put*. One can be first intimidated by the army of roughly two hundred English irregulars waiting out there, ready to eat into your brain. However, they are not as scary as you first think: the irregular forms often look similar to the original verb (except for good old *went*), and there are several identifiable patterns in how to form and predict the forms: *brought, bought, caught* and *taught*; *driven, ridden* and *written*, and so on.

There are only eleven irregular verbs in Irish against the two hundred English ones. But be under no illusions: they will easily beat the English ones, you just wait and see. For a start, the three forms of Irish verbs are present–past–future, not present–past–perfect. The past and, in some extreme cases, the future form do not resemble the root word (the infinitive) at all. Had

I not warned you beforehand, you would have hardly thought that *téigh, chuaigh* and *rachaidh* were in any way connected, still less that they were forms of the same verb, but I am afraid they are. Ladies and gentlemen, this is the Irish verb 'to go', present–past–future!

This is not the end of the story though. The past tense form hides even darker secrets. Try to say 'I didn't go' or 'Did you go?' Simple, you would say, just take the past form *chuaigh* and add the negative or the question word. *Ní chuaigh mé* and *An chuaigh mé?* Ooooops. Wrong. I am afraid the verb 'to go' decided to produce separate forms, just in case. *Ní dheachaigh* for 'I didn't go' and *An ndeachaigh?* for 'Did you go?'

Some other irregular verbs are a bit tamer. For example, 'to come' has the decency to start with the same letter in all three forms – *tar, tháinig, tiocfaidh* – and to not change its appearance for questions and negations. The majority are a mixed bag, with one form being close to the initial and the other running amok: *faigh* ('to get') is a modest *fuair* in the past but explodes into *gheobhaidh* in the future.

Don't you think eleven is quite enough? I definitely do. No need to compete with the two hundred in English. Quality, not quantity.

Culture Pool

Irish irregulars are so unlike their European peers that they prefer keeping their own company. Only one verb – 'to come' in its future form – has made an appearance on the international arena and gotten quite famous in certain circles. If you go to Belfast, you will surely learn about 'The Troubles' of the late 1960s–1990s and see the many murals with political messages. One of the most famous slogans was written in Irish by the members of the Irish Republican Army (IRA), who fought for a united Ireland. It reads *Tiocfaidh Ár Lá* ('our day will come'). Now it also appears on political souvenirs (T-shirts, cups, etc.) which you can find in Dublin in a shop run by the left-wing nationalist Sinn Féin party (see Picture 25).

27 | PREPOSITION MONSTERS

Another part of speech which can wreck anyone's brain is Irish prepositions.

When we talk about actions, how do we know who performs them? In many European languages we simply use an appropriate pronoun like *I, he, they,* etc., plus a verb. Some languages like German or Russian also change the verb by adding personal endings to it. 'I buy' in German will be *ich kaufe,* 'you buy' – *du kaufst,* he buys – *er kauft* and so on. The Irish language has personal endings too. The problem is that it has chosen not to bother the verbs too much (they are busy enough as it is) and put the burden on prepositions. Have you ever heard of prepositions which have personal endings to mark 'I', 'you', 'he', etc? Sounds crazy. Well, Irish, Welsh, Scottish Gaelic, Manx and Breton (the other surviving Celtic languages) are the only European languages which do such things to their beloved prepositions.

Just imagine, instead of learning simply *in, on, with, at,* etc. you have to learn seven forms for each preposition and use an appropriate form every time you speak. To give you a flavour of what Irish prepositions are like, here is a table for the preposition *le* ('with'):

Le ('with')	
liom *(with me)*	**linn** *(with us)*
leat *(with you)*	**libh** *(with you, plural)*
leis *(with him)*	
léi *(with her)*	**leo** *(with them)*

97

Now imagine a naughty Irish-speaking child in a big Irish-speaking family, constantly changing his mind about who he will go in the car with. *I'll go with you! No, I'll go with her! No, with him!* Let him be naughty; he has done his penance already, switching between those preposition forms like mad: *Rachaidh mé **leat**! Rachaidh mé **léi**! Rachaidh mé **leis**!*

There are fifteen common prepositions which change in this way in modern Irish.[28] It leaves the speakers with just over one hundred different forms to remember.

Culture Pool

Irish grammar is so crazy, and learning the language so brain-wrecking yet fun, that there is a comedy show about it. An Irish-American stand-up comedian, Des Bishop, describes his own experience of learning Irish in a hilarious show called *In the Name of the Fada*, a *fada* being an accent mark above some Irish vowels.

---

[28] According to the grammar reference *Gramadach gan Stró*.

28 | P.S. THERE IS ♥ AT ME ON YOU

Despite the linguistic complexity, which would require a mathematical brain to master it, Irish is also a deeply poetic language. Instead of just labelling an action or an object, it often describes it in several words, and prepositions come in very handy here. For a start, there is no verb 'to have', and you need to say 'there is X at me' instead.[29]

You do not call your parents; you *put a call on them.* And you do that to show that you love them? Not quite, but that *there is love at you on them.* Have you forgotten to do it? Well, not an Irishman, he has *done forgetting on it.* Do you like coffee? Yes, coffee is *good with me.*

And this is not the limit either. My favourites are nouns where the language's poetic nature runs wild. A wolf is called *mac tíre,* 'the son of the earth'; a spider *damhán alla,* 'little wild ox'; and the pupil in one's eye turns out to be 'the son of iris'. Do you like jellyfish? The Irish don't either, so they called it *smugairle róin* – 'seal's snot' in other words. Here is another word with an attitude. When jazz arrived, its frivolous sharp changes of tone might have been too much for the more conservative Irish ear used to traditional music. Feeling a bit suspicious of the newcomer, the Irish called it *snagcheol,* 'hiccup music'. And in case, having heard

---

[29] In fact, Irish is not an exception here. There are some languages which lack the verb 'to have' or at least do not make use of it even if they have it; for example Russian, which, funnily enough, uses a construction very similar to the Irish one.

all this, you fall for the beauty of the Irish language and decide to study it, there is a poetic phrase made especially for you: no way will you become students of Irish – you will be *mic léinn*, 'sons of learning'.

To end this section on a truly poetic note, if you want to address your loved one in Irish you will say *a chuisle mo chroí*, which is no more or less than 'the pulse of my heart'. How deep down indeed one's love can grow!

29 | ANY PLANS FOR THE DAY OF FASTING?

Apart from being poets and warriors, the ancient Irish were also eager pagans and developed a complex system of beliefs in the spirits of nature and the afterlife. However, shortly after 432, the year St Patrick's apostolic mission began, they became devoted Christians and have remained such as a nation up until very recently. The religious predisposition of the Irish found its way into their language and stayed there, reminding us of their religious traditions both past and present. Pagan and Christian beliefs have always been interwoven in Irish culture, which is also reflected in the language.

Our departure point is the names for days of the week. Saturday, Monday and Tuesday represent pre-Christian beliefs and are all derived from Latin. *Satharn* (Saturday) is named after Saturn or Chronos, the father of Zeus/Jupiter in the Graeco-Roman tradition. *Luan*, like its English counterpart Monday, is the day of the moon, while *Máirt* (Tuesday) honours the god of war, Mars.

Sunday, Wednesday, Thursday and Friday, however, derive their names from Christianity. *Domhnach* (Sunday) comes from the Latin *Dies Dominica*, which means 'the day of the Lord', whereas Wednesday, Thursday and Friday are native Irish words which reflect the Christian tradition of fasting. Wednesday and Friday are the fasting days of the week, Wednesday being the day when Judas betrayed Jesus and Friday being the day Jesus was crucified. To mark this tradition, the Irish called Wednesday *Céadaoin* ('the first fast'), Thursday *Déardaoin* ('between the fasts') and Friday simply *Aoine* ('fast').

Irish names for months display a more diverse picture in terms of their origins. Arguably, the most famous month is November – *Samhain* – which bears the name of an ancient Celtic festival when spirits were believed to enter the human world. Samhain celebrations, evolving but persisting through centuries, gave birth to the modern Halloween. Two other months – May (*Bealtaine*) and August (*Lúnasa*) – are also the names of Celtic pagan festivals, the first one being again connected with spirits coming into the world, and the second with a Celtic god, Lugh. Yet another month is named after its main festivity, Christmas. The Irish word for both December and Christmas is *Nollaig*, which comes from the Latin word *natalicia*, meaning 'birthday entertainment' or 'birthday party'. Nollaig, the month of the birthday party, celebrates in its name the birth of Jesus Christ. The rest of the months are either of Latin origin (mainly names of the Roman gods) or native Irish, but they do not carry any overt religious meaning.

Back in the early days when Christianity was in its prime in Ireland, the best you could wish a person was God's presence and blessing. So, to this day, to say 'Hello' in Irish, we use the phrase *Dia duit,* which means 'God to you'. The answer is *Dia is Muire duit*, which is 'God and Mary to you'. Sometimes, if someone is feeling especially generous, he can answer *Dia, Muire agus Pádraig duit* – it's no harm having the blessing of St Patrick, the patron saint, on top of that of God Himself and the Virgin Mary.

The Irish language provides blessings or good wishes for every side of life.[30] You can call on God to give someone a long life (*Go saolaí Dia thú*), a bit of help (*Nár rabhair riamh gan chúnamh*), good health (*Go bhfága Dia do shláinte agat*) and some sense (*Go dtuga Dia ciall duit*) – that last one is a bit harsh, isn't it? Or you can tell your friend that you sincerely hope God will never torment them (*Nár chrá Dia choíche thú*). There is also a very inventive one: *may you never wed again* (*Nár phósair go brách arís*). Sounds like a curse, doesn't it? Just think for a moment. It is actually a poetic way of wishing that a married couple stay together till death do them part. There are some blessings which do not involve calling on God directly. They are more of a wish which will come true with the help of God. There are two very well-known ones which most Irish people know by heart. *Go n-éirí an bóthar leat* ('may the road rise up to you') can mean either wishing a literal safe journey, or a symbolic journey towards success ('good luck' in more prosaic terms). The other blessing I wanted to introduce is often said on important dates of the year (someone's birthday, Christmas, St Patrick's Day, etc.). It can be easily used in an English conversation. For example, just after a birthday toast, someone might add thoughtfully: *Go mbeirimid beo ag an am seo arís* – 'may we all be alive at this time next year'.

You might think that with the advance of more scep-tical thinking nowadays, Irish blessings might have lost their purpose. Not really. They are a common way of saying 'Happy Easter/Christmas/St Patrick's Day,

---

[30] The blessings discussed below are translations from Irish. The proverbs and their translations have been taken from Garry Bannister's book *Proverbs in Irish* (pp. 48–50).

etc.' *Beannachtaí na Féile Pádraig* – 'The blessings of the feast of Patrick on you'. Sounds very solid indeed. *Beannacht* ('blessing') is a shrewd word. Having secured its place on cards for various occasions, it has also jumped on the bandwagon of modern technology and become one of the ways to sign off an email in Irish: *Le gach beannacht* ('with every blessing'). Another no less religious one is *Le gach dea-ghuí* ('with every good prayer/wish'). The English equivalents would be the much more neutral 'kind regards' or 'best wishes'.

There is a thin line between love and hate however. Give it a moment, and instead of a nice blessing you will be suddenly looking for a good old swearword. As we all know, though, offensive language is impolite. In Christianity, it is not just impolite but is considered a sin. Since the Irish language was evolving under a strong Christian influence, it did not really form properly offensive (i.e. obscene) language of its own. Instead, curses (often religious or death-related) of an unbeatably expressive nature were created.[31] Enjoy:

- *Go dtachta an diabhal thú!* ('May the devil choke you!')
- *D'anam don scian!* ('Your soul to the knife!')
- *Ná raibh Ifreann lán go raibh tú ann!* ('May Hell not be full until you arrive!')
- *Lá breá ag do chairde – do d'adhlacadh!* ('May your friends have a fine day – burying you!')

---

[31] A wider selection of these curses can be found in many sources, both in print and online. I have used a selection from Garry Bannister's *Proverbs in Irish* (pp. 93–94), www.focloir.ie, www.gaelchultur.com/en/phrase_of_the_day.aspx and www.irishcentral.com/homepage/a-guide-to-cursing-in-irish-for-st-patricks-day-get-your-irish-up-with-these-phrases-as-gaelige-198433411-237783261.

- *Go n-ithe an cat thú, is go n-ithe an diabhal an cat!* ('May the cat eat you and may the devil eat the cat!')
- *Briseadh agus brú ar do chnámha!* ('Breaking and crushing on your bones!')
- *Tochas gan ingne ort!* ('May you have an itch and no nails!')
- *Go n-ithe an cancar thú!* ('May grumpiness devour you!')
- *Go gcuire sé saill ort!* ('May it make you fat!')
- *Céile leice leisciúil léanmhar chugat!* ('May your spouse be a lazy, unfortunate idiot!')

Later on, in modern times, the idea of contemporary English swearwords was imported into Irish. In some cases, older curses took on the meaning of a vulgar English expression. For example, a common Irish equivalent of *F*ck off*, is a rather tame *Téigh dtí diabhail* ('Go to the devil'). The exclamation *F*ck!* is also often translated as *A dhiabhail!* There also exists a Gaelicised form of this English swearword (*focáil*) but again it is more likely to be a modern borrowing from English rather than the product of the Irish language. It seems to me that the most common practice among Irish speakers nowadays is to simply insert English swearwords into Irish speech whenever they feel the need to be rude.

Ironically, the idea of swearing in Irish proved to be very dear to the heart of the tourist business. Every second (if not single) tourist shop will have a T-shirt, a card, a magnet, or even a piece of underwear saying *Póg mo thóin*, which is a translation of the long-established (since 1705) English expression 'Kiss my arse' (see Picture 26). The obsession with this phrase is still a mystery to me. Is it there to symbolise the mischievous nature of the Irish? Still, it seems that the language with the oldest native literary tradition in Europe can do better than being advertised to the international public through an obscenity.

30 | THE WORLD THROUGH GREEN-COLOURED GLASSES

The abundance of references to religion in everyday Irish is a fine example of how a language can reflect the worldview of its people. Just look at the wordstock of a language more closely, compare it to the languages you know, and you will see what a different picture each language paints. It will become clear what is important for its people, what nature they are surrounded by, what their ways of life have been, what difficulties they have lived through over the centuries; you might even get a peep into what their philosophy of life is.[32]

All this talk may have rung a bell with you by now, and you will say, yes, it is like the Eskimo languages with their numerous words for describing different types of snow. That's a famous one all right; just google 'Eskimo languages' and the second suggested search term will be 'Eskimo languages snow'. The Eskimo people may never grow tired of creating numerous words for snow, but the Irish are not far behind with some say 23, some 50, others boldly go as high as 100 words and expressions to describe … potatoes. Yes! Every size and shape is accounted for, every way of cooking it (you had to be inventive when there was

---

[32]   There is a whole theory in linguistics which talks about this kind of thing. It was first formulated by Herder and Von Humboldt, German scholars, early romantics and nationalists, at the end of the eighteenth and beginning of the nineteenth centuries. It was later developed by two American linguists, Sapir and Whorf, in the 1930s–1940s.

not much other food around), and even every fault is meticulously documented – from a potato ruined by exposure to sunlight (*práta gréine*, literally 'potato of the sun') to a frost-bitten one (*práta seaca*, 'potato of the frost').[33] I will spare you the pain (or deprive you of the joy) of going through the whole list in Irish. The only other word I want you to know is the standard neutral word for potatoes – *prátaí*. Just in case you are looking for a bite to eat somewhere out West.

All those lovely potatoes, big and small, grow in lush green fields. The green of the fields, the green of the dreamy hills, the green of the sunlit sea, the green of the soccer team jerseys. The Emerald Isle. Indeed, green has always been the dominant colour of this land, something people cast their eyes on 365 days a year. So they noticed it was never the same. The Irish language was there, ready to lend its speakers support in talking about the colour of their land. Your fields and lawns are *glas,* that fine, deep, calming sort of green. So are Irish eyes: *glas,* green with that melancholy pinch of grey. You will never paint your fence *glas* though; neither will you get a *carr glas.* For that artificially bright green the Irish language reserved the word *uaine.* Finally, when you look over the Atlantic on a fresh sunny morning, its crystal clear waters are *gorm*: green with a hint of blue.

The waters surrounding Ireland are another vital component of Irish life. Interestingly enough, whether speaking Irish or English, the Irish do not make a distinction between the sea and the ocean, and just call it *the sea,* although Ireland has the Irish *Sea* to the east and the Atlantic *Ocean* to the west. It seems

---

[33] Credit for the list of potato words go to the author of a potato-dedicated blog, *The Daily Spud*, at www.thedailyspud.com.

that people living side by side with this natural power see it as one: either it is the sea or the ocean, it feeds them, it is calm and pleasant to fish and swim in, or it is dangerously furious and merciless to anyone attempting to tame it. You go for a swim *san fharraige,* that is 'in the sea'. *Farraige* is one of three words which describe the vast waters around Ireland, but it pulls more than its share of weight. It originally means 'sea' but is used in, roughly speaking, 80 per cent of everyday conversations about the sea and the ocean. You will see numerous B&Bs on both the east and the west coasts called *Cois Farraige* (literally 'beside the sea'). The Aran ferry fleet owns a delightful passanger boat with an open-roof upper deck called *Ceol na Farraige* – the music of the sea (never mind that it is crossing the Atlantic).

There is another word – *muir.* It seems to have been bullied by *farraige* into doing all the dirty work, that is forming a part of various phrases rather than being a free-floating word. All the official names of seas take *muir: Meánmhuir* and *Muir Chairib,* the Mediterranean and the Caribbean Seas. *Muir* is also fond of being the second component in phrases like 'X of the sea' or 'Sea Y' in its genetive form *mara.* Marine animals and plants are *ainmhithe agus plandaí mara;* when they become seafood they are called *bia mara.* The same goes for seabirds, coastguards and numerous animals which, instead of having a separate name, are called 'X of the sea': the knife of the sea (a razor clam), the cross of the sea (a starfish), the life of the sea (plankton), the pig of the sea (porpoise) or the cow of the sea, which is, thankfully, a sea cow in English. *Muir* has also left its trace in the name of a very special region in the West of Ireland which I mentioned to you before:

*Conne**mara*** (or *Conamara* in Irish). A long time ago a big tribe called the *Conmhaicne* owned lands in the West. The branch of this tribe which had control over the lands by the sea came to be known as *Conmhaicne of the Sea, Conmhaicne Mara*, which later turned into the name of these lands – Connemara.

The third word is reserved for the nerdy types who cannot stand calling the ocean 'the sea'. *Aigéan* is not really used in speech. It means 'ocean' and ocean only, and might be heard at conferences or read in books concerned with geography.

Interestingly, both *farraige* and *muir*, the functioning sea words, so to speak, are, grammatically, feminine nouns. It may reflect the same tendency as machinery and ships being traditionally refered to as 'she' in English. The suggested explanation behind the English tradition is that it was traditionally men who looked after machines, so they associated caring for machines with caring for women, and talked about them using feminine pronouns. We may only guess that a similar thing might have happened with *farraige* and *muir* as at least in the old times the sea was always on the minds of Irish men; they were forever going to sea, trying to tame and comprehend its often capricious nature.

Grammatical gender, however boring it may sound, is a powerful tool, capable of labelling something once and forever. And if that label is not a kindly one, hard luck. Here is what the Irish language did to take revenge on its historical rival, the English language. The names of all languages in Irish are feminine except for one: *Béarla* (English). Hardly a coincidence, is it?[34]

---

[34] A linguistic explanation behind it is that *Béarla* was a masculine noun which simply meant 'language' in Old Irish. It started to

You don't always have to be that implicit though. There are much more straightforward ways of expressing your views on life, for example proverbs.[35] Irish, a language with an ancient poetic tradition, has a rich stock of those. Some of them are more popular than the others, and many a proverb has made it into Irish textbooks and, hopefully, students' brains.

There are a number of proverbs shared by English and Irish (as well as some other languages). However, Irish proverbs are that little bit different from their English counterparts, with a sprinkle of local colour. When in Rome, do as the Romans do. Fair enough, the Irish agree, but they have got an example closer to home: all those little islands off the coast of Ireland are special enough, so *When on the island, accept the customs of the island.* A bird in the hand is worth two in the bush. However, fish is more valuable for the Irish, so the Irish version goes *A trout in the hand is worth a salmon in the pool.* If you are being awkward, like an elephant in a china shop, in Ireland you will be labelled *A fisherman in a tailor's shop.* That is indeed much closer to everyday life. Here is another maritime variation: *A tree has to be knocked down to put up sails.* You can't make an omelette without breaking eggs, that is. Since there are no wolves in Ireland and foxes are farmers' enemy number one, what we have got here is *Foxes in a lamb's skin,* lurking around the place.

A lot of Irish proverbs, however, do not have direct parallels in English but nevertheless they very well

---

be used in relation to the English *language*, as in *the language* (you decide if this usage was full of admiration or fear and anger).

[35] The proverbs discussed below are translations from Irish. The proverbs and their translations have been taken from Garry Bannister's book *Proverbs in Irish.*

reflect the Irish view of the world. Animals form a big part of the Irish expressive repertoire. Cows, pigs, hens and lambs, the key animals in Irish farming, are prominent in Irish proverbs. Strangely enough, cows seem to be reserved for talking about weaknesses and unimportant things. A harmless fight is *a fight between bald cows,* whereas the coward's way out is *Weak cows run downhill.* Pigs are absolutely despised. You can be *as bold as a pig, as ugly as a pig, as fat as a pig, as dirty as a pig* and *as shameless as a pig.* Have they really deserved all that? Animals were proving to be such a helpful way of making sense of the world that women were viewed through the animal prism too, so, as the harsh old saying goes, *there are three kinds of women: a woman as shameless as a pig, a woman as contrary as a hen, and a woman as gentle as a lamb.* That's not very nice, is it?

A great love for tea, so typical of the Irish nation, has also found its way into the language. That complicated love–hate relationship some have with their nearest and dearest ('can't live with them, can't live without them') the Irish have with their tea: *dead from tea and dead without it.* Also, *the best time to drink tea is any time at all.*

However, deep down, there might be something else as dear to the Irish heart as the tea itself: their native language. This importance of language as a symbol and a part of what a nation is, is reflected in one of the most famous and used Irish proverbs. *Tír gan teanga – tír gan anam.* A country without a language is a country without a soul. One could say that the whole Irish revitalisation campaign has been happening under the banner of this influencial proverb.

31 | ENGLISH WITH AN IRISH FLAVOUR

Even if the Irish were not able to keep their language alive and well after the disastrous nineteenth century, they managed to pass on a little bit of that Irish soul to the English they spoke.

Indeed, if languages are in continual contact, they will eventually start borrowing words and sometimes even grammatical structures from one another. The English language has been in Ireland for over 800 years, and in direct contact with Irish from the sixteenth century onwards. Such a long coexistence of the two languages makes mutual influence inevitable. English developed a distinctive variety usually called Irish English (just like British English, American English, etc.)[36] From the beginning of the twentieth century, Irish English spoken by well-educated middle-class speakers started forming the local standard. In its more colloquial and colourful variant, Irish English is associated with working-class people and the country-side. What made Irish English a distinctive variety? You will say the influence of the Irish language, of course, when the majority of the population were switching to English but still spoke it as a second language. Well, yes and no. Scholars have been debating this question

---

[36] You may come across other terms like Anglo-Irish or Hiberno-English, which sometimes mean the same as Irish English; in other cases they refer to the sub-types of Irish English. Many contemporary scholars recommend using the term 'Irish English' to avoid further confusion.

for decades. There are certain features of Irish English which did come from Irish, whereas other ones are the relics of seventeeth- and eighteenth-century English, or the result of historical language changes.

Nevertheless, we can be quite certain that the English spoken in Ireland owes much of its expressive nature, numerous religious exclamations and some dialectal expressions to the Irish language. It is common to hear Irish people use references to God. Is someone in trouble? *God help him.* Have you heard something scary on the news? *God bless us and save us!* Did someone scare or surprise you? *Jeeesus!* That fellow looks miserable – *poor devil;* maybe *there is sorrow **on** him* – sure *he **is after hearing** bad news.* Do you remember how much the Irish language likes prepositional phrases? Well, as you can see, some of them made it into colloquial Irish English speech.[37]

Apart from prepositions, the Irish language has developed a deep love for the word *féin,* meaning 'self'. When you speak Irish, it is good manners to stick *féin* to personal pronouns like 'I' or 'you' from time to time. Irish English has keenly picked up the habit, and people started using a lot of *myself, yourself,* etc. even if nothing more than *I* or *you* is needed. *Any tea for yourself? I think it's a good idea. What about yourselves?* The imagination of Irish people has no boundaries, so they started using *himself* and *herself* to talk about their husbands/ wives/girlfriends/boyfriends. *We might go but I need to talk to himself first.*

Irish English has also inherited the friendliness and affection which developed in traditionally close-knit communities. The Irish language has a lot of endearing

---

[37] Not all distinctive prepositional usages definitely come from Irish but these two are likely candidates.

words which are used with family members as well as friends or even strangers. You might remember one of them, *a chuisle mo chroí* ('the pulse of my heart'). Others include a shorter version *a chuisle*, as well as *a stór* or *a stóirín* ('treasure' or 'little treasure'). Irish English did not preserve this variety of endearements but resorted to the single 'love' instead. *Sorry love* your collegue may apologise for accidentally getting in your way; *Here you are love* as your local shopkeeper hands you over a carton of milk. *Where are you going love?* enquires the bus driver and prints out your ticket. Where there is affection, there is a blessing. Blessings are not as abundant in English as in Irish but there are a couple of them that got carried over. *God bless* is still a common way of saying goodbye, especially in the country. If you are discussing someone's misfortune or even simple awkwardness, you might as well be as kind as you possibly can and insert that *God love him/her* somewhere in the middle of the sentence.

Some Irish words, however, made it beyond the local form of English and secured a firm place in standard English vocabulary. One of the words which the English colonisers picked up quite early on (1505) was *bog*, as there is no shortage of them in Ireland. The Irish for 'bog' is *bogach*,[38] whereas the actual Irish word *bog*, which gave birth to *bogach*, means 'soft'. Fair enough. There were *bogach go leor* in Ireland, as we said: a lot of bogs. A sufficient number. The English liked that other word too and borrowed it around 1675. There are bogs *galore* in this country, they used to say. Not only the Irish nature but the Irish way of life seemed very different to the English. The Irish used to wear

---

[38] There are also other words for 'bog' in modern Irish, for example *portach*.

115

breeches of their own fashion which they called *triub-
has.*[39] The English started calling them *trousers* and
got to love the word so much that they binned their
own word for similar clothes and adopted *trousers* as
the main label for that type of clothing around 1676.
The Irish also distinguished themselves by wearing
very rough shoes. They called them just 'shoes', *bróga.*
The English picked up the word and started calling
these Irish-fashioned shoes *brogues.* At the beginning
of the twentieth century, when people developed an
interest in hobbies like sport, hiking and camping,
manufacturers decided to produce special rough shoes
for those kinds of outings. Of course they called them
brogues.

Every good manufacturer needs to advertise. If
you want to advertise, you need a memorable slogan.
Where do you get a slogan? Obviously you go to
Ireland. Irish chieftains of old were really into fighting,
first among themselves and later against the invaders.
Each clan had a distinctive battle cry which they called
sluagh gairm, 'the cry of the army'. The English had no
choice but to call this terrifying cry by its name: they
labelled it *slogorne* around 1513. As time went by and
the chieftains lost their power and glory, the word was
not needed anymore. However, the English went on to
squeeze a new meaning out of it. As early as 1704 the
Irish *sluagh gairm* became *slogan* in the modern sense
of the word.

Once you have got your slogan, there is one more
thing you need – an eye-catching logo. The Irish have
got that one covered too – come here for St Patrick's

---

[39] Modern Irish has two words for trousers: *bríste* and *triús,* as
well as *treabhsar* – trousers – which have come full circle from
English back into Irish.

day or simply wander into an Irish souvenir shop and there it is, leaping at you – the famous Irish shamrock. We just seem to accept that for some reason the clover plant is called *shamrock* when we talk about all things Irish. Why *shamrock* though, and not *clover*? Well, it actually IS a clover. The Irish word for 'clover' is *seamair*. To show that extra Irish affection towards the national plant, the Irish started calling it 'a little clover', *seamróg*.

Culture Pool

Many of us know Bram Stoker as the author of *Dracula*. However, as an Irish writer he was an expert not only in vampires but also in Irish English. His early novel *The Snake's Path* (1890), set in a village in the West of Ireland, is full of colourful English speech heavily affected by the Irish language. Whether you are interested in a portion of exaggerated Irish English or you feel like a love story between a refined Englishman and a peasant Irish girl, *The Snake's Path* is a novel to check out.

IRISH WITH AN ENGLISH FLAVOUR | 32

As English was growing and absorbing the linguistic imperfections of Irish speakers, Irish itself was declining – in terms of the number of speakers and as a language system. The linguistic tragedy of Irish was that its development as the language of the nation was terminated about 200 years ago. While other European languages were forming national oral and written standards, Irish was turning into a group of dialects used mainly by poorly educated peasants. As a result, Irish has never developed a national standard in a natural way. A standard variety had to be artificially constructed in the 1940s and 1950s by combining features of the three main dialects. Moreover, having been primarily the language of the countryside spoken by farmers and labourers, Irish did not rise up to the ever-growing complexity of cotemporary human thought and invention. As a result, the revived Irish of the twentieth century had to borrow the vocabulary necessary to keep up with contemporary life: words and structures for modern concepts, abstract ideas, scientific terms and even swearwords.

You should have no difficulty recognising such words as *fón, criú, ceamara* or *cliceáil*. They are only *phone, crew, camera* and the verb *to click*. Sometimes, the Irish spelling goes hard on English loanwords and makes them follow the local fashion for extra obscure letters. Try to recognise these English words 'colonised' by Irish: *haigh, beidhsicil, siogairéad, suipéar* and *siopa*. A bit puzzled? No worries, here are the answers: *hi, bicycle, cigarette, supper* and *shop*.

So far, so good. However, with no Irish you will hardly guess what *idirlíon, griangraf, ríomhaire* or *rúnaí* are. They were also borrowed but in a subtler way. Only the idea of how to construct a word was copied but the elements used for construction were native. This is what linguists call a 'calque'. The words above mean 'inter-net', 'photo-graph', compute-r' and 'secret-ary' respectively. *Íoslódáil* is a nice hybrid. The logic of the English 'download' is used, with the native Irish word for 'down' (*íos*) merged with an English loanword ('load'). For other computer or technical terms Irish uses its own native words by giving them a new meaning, just as the English word 'attachment' acquired a new meaning of virtual rather than physical connection. However, Irish, full of poetic expressions for everyday things, felt a nudge to spice up that dry technical vocabulary. What do we do with 'spam'? Some people said, let's leave it, it's short and handy. So they put it in the dictionary. Others, however, said, wait, we have a lovely word for all sorts of rubbish – *turscar*. It originally meant 'seaweed which has been washed up on the shore and is of no use', just lying there rotting. What an apt description for those intrusive and often unpleasant emails. Dear spammers, stop sending me rotten seaweed please.

If you have to tolerate unpleasant things in Irish, an English phrasal verb comes to help. Irish takes the English *put up with* and translates it word by word (*put – up – with: cuir – suas – le*) into Irish. There are more phrasal verbs like that in Irish which basically follow the English template and are used exactly in the same context as the English ones.

119

Despite many established calques for new phenomena (like *idirlíon*), it is common practice in Irish speech (including fluent speakers) to use an English word to express a complex contemporary concept. For example, there is a long boring word, *dlúthdhiosca*, which the authors of *The Irish–English Computer Dictionary* came up with. However, I bet most Irish speakers would rather use *CD* instead and then happily carry on in Irish. This trend, despite some people's criticism, seems to me to be a sign of a living language, trying to adapt to a rapidly changing way of life. If Irish speakers are agile enough to make a quick switch and easily get back into the flow of their native tongue, it is a sign of being comfortable in that language rather than a lack of proper knowledge. *Das Baby, das Meeting, download-en, der Job and die Performance* haven't killed German yet, so there might be some hope for Irish as well!

Picture 20

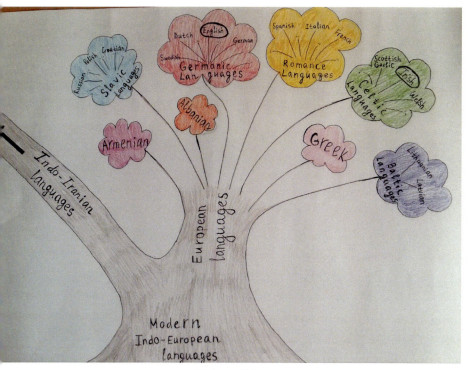

Picture 21

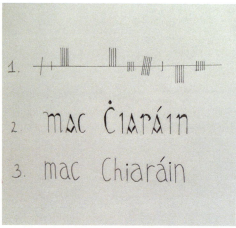

1.

2. mac Ċiaráin

3. mac Chiaráin

Picture 22

Picture 23

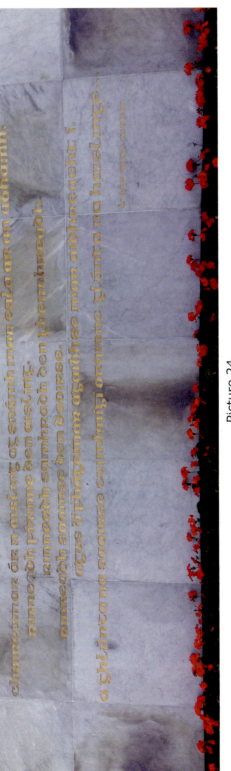

Picture 24

Picture 25

Picture 26

PART III

IRISH:
A SMALL LANGUAGE IN
A BIG WORLD

Slowly but surely, through ups and downs, the Irish language is catching up with modern life and is even going international. Its latest achievement in that department has been securing the status of one of the official working languages of the EU in 2002. This means loads of document translation and interpreting of Irish MEPs (should they choose to speak Irish) for the less fluent members of the European Parliament. Dry officialdom – we won't dwell on it any longer. Instead, we will look at some more exciting ways in which Irish has made its presence known to the wider world.

33 | THE WATER OF LIFE

Many of you would say you could bet anything that never in your lives have you used a single word of Irish. If I told you that you definitely have, several times, dozens of times, maybe even (dare I say) hundreds of times, your natural reaction would be to write me off as a nutcase. But are you really sure there is no Irish word lurking in the bends of your brain?

In the late sixteenth century, when Elizabeth I was the Queen of England, active colonisation of Ireland and North America by the English began. Expeditions to explore and conquer new lands were undertaken; colonisers returned to England with stories and samples of local ways of life. One of the culinary discoveries brought back from Ireland was a curious drink which had been distilled there for centuries (at least since 1405). The Irish called it *uisce beatha* in their native language, which meant 'the water of life'. Uisce beatha started to be exported to the English court, and the exportation continued ever since, spreading to other countries with time. Nowadays this drink is on the shelves of off-licences and duty frees all over the world.

First, the English borrowed the full name of the drink and wrote it down as one word, trying to copy the original pronunciation. Early examples of the written forms in English sources include *vskebeaghe*[40] (1581), *vsquebach* (1658), *usquebagh* (1682), *usquebaugh*

---

[40] 'u' and 'v' were used interchangeably.

(1706–1707) and other variations. Later, the second word, or at this stage the second part, '*beatha*', started to fall off, allowing *uisce* to turn into the most internationally used and famous word of the Irish language. *Uisce* became *whiskey*.

Culture Pool

Everyone knows about whiskey but not everyone knows about its cousin, *poitín*. It is described by some people as the strongest alcoholic drink in the world, as it can reach 90 per cent spirit concentration. Basically, poitín is a kind of homemade whiskey distilled from barley or potatoes. It is said that people in Ireland started making poitín as early as the sixth century. It takes its name from the Irish word for 'pot' – *pota* – plus the diminutive suffix –*ín*; literally, 'the small pot'. Poitín was illegal until 1997 and has traditionally been associated with underground distilling in the West of Ireland and, through that, to a certain extent, with the Irish language. It is no surprise then that the first Irish language feature film, made in 1978, was about poitín-making in Connemara and was called, you'll never guess, *Poitín!*

If all this poitín talk has got you intrigued and you are wondering where you could see (and maybe taste) the drink, I have some good news for you. Milder poitín (40–60 per cent proof) can be produced legally now and is available in supermarkets as well as in pubs and bars.

34 | WHAT'S IN A SURNAME?

It is not only a drink that the Irish language can offer the world. Quite a few Irish names and surnames, having been tamed and adopted by the English language, have gone on to conquer the world.

Once upon a time, before the British tred on Irish soil, there were family clans in Ireland known by Gaelic surnames of *Ó Cinnéide*, *Ó Brosnacháin*, *Ó Conaire*, *Ó Leannáin*, *Ó hEaghra*, *Mac Dhomhnaill* and *Mac Aonghusa*. Time went by, the British influence grew stronger, and, over time, the colonisers as well as the owners of these family names started to simplify them to suit the English ear. Emigration to Britain and America over the last two or three centuries gave this anglicising tendency an extra push. As a result, those initial *Ó*s and *Mac*s often got thrown away. In other cases, they were kept but slightly modified. However sad it is that people were forced to change their names and emigrate, some good came out of it. The Irish can be proud that their ancient surnames were made world-famous by US President John *Kennedy*, Hollywood stars Pierce *Brosnan* and Sean *Connery*, the un*beatle*ble (great pun!) John *Lennon*, an iconic film character Scarlett *O'Hara*, the *McDonald* brothers in America who cashed in on the idea of fast food, and of course the beer brewer who gave its name to the 'black stuff' usually referred to as *Guinness*.

Although Kennedy, Brosnan and Guinness have lost their *Ó*s and *Mac*s, there are quite a few surnames which haven't, so you might as well learn what these prefixes mean. *Ó* (as well as its other form *Uí*) means 'descendant of' or simply 'from', so the surname used to identify which family or clan a person was descended from. Which Scarlett? From the *Hara* (or *Eaghra* if you prefer) family.

Mac, like *Ó*, once used to be something like an identification label. *Mac* means 'son' in Irish, so the surname originally meant 'son of ...', for example Mac Chormaic was 'son of Cormac', and later on turned into McCormac. The 1169 invasion brought the Anglo-Norman version of Mac – *fils de* (or *fitz*) – which gave birth to surnames like Fitzgerald and Fitzpatrick.

There are also separate female versions of *Ó* and *Mac* – *Ní* and *Nic* respectively. *Ní* stands for *iníon uí*, 'daughter of the decendant of ...' and *Nic* 'daughter of the son of ...'. These are traditional surname prefixes for unmarried girls and women. When and if they got married, their lives got busier and their surnames longer. To change her surname to *Ó Conaill*, a newlywed would have to call herself 'the wife of *Ó* Conaill' – *Bean Uí Chonaill*, or simply *Uí Chonaill*. Taking a surname starting with *Mac* would mean acquiring the lengthy title of 'wife of the son of ...' – *bean Mhic* or just *Mhic*. However, unlike *Ó* and *Mac* themselves, their feminine forms are not that widely used nowadays, unless a woman consciously chooses to be known under the Irish form of her family name.

Culture Pool

People all over the world may admire Scarlett *O'Hara* from *Gone with the Wind* but not all of them will notice how many Irish references there are in this story. Scarlett O'Hara is the daughter of an Irish emigrant to the United States, Gerard O'Hara. The story takes place in the 1860s, so we can assume that her father was one of the many Irish people who emigrated in the wake of or during the Great Famine. If you make the Irish connection and remember how the Irish were robbed of their land, evicted from their houses and pushed into the regions of the country where nothing would grow, much of what Gerard O'Hara says makes more sense. He famously gets annoyed at his daughter for not caring about their land and exclaims that 'land is the only thing in the world ... worth working for, worth fighting for – worth dying for.'[41]

As you may remember, the land or the estate Gerard O'Hara owned in the US was called *Tara*. It is quite a name if you look into Irish history. The Hill of Tara is an open space in County Meath, Ireland. It used to be the seat of the High King of Ireland from ancient times until the eleventh century. All that is left of it now are separate stones, forts and trench-shaped earthworks. The shapes of the site make sense only when looked at from the air. The thousand-year-old Stone of Destiny might be the highlight of your visit to Tara. It is said to scream when the true king of Ireland touches it. It is worth a try (it didn't work for me, so I had to go book-writing). I will ask you only one thing now. Never confuse the Irish Tara with the O'Hara's estate. I have heard several people quite seriously exclaim when they saw my pictures of *the* Tara: 'Oh, and where is the O'Hara's mansion?' Well, the answer is

---

[41]   Margaret Mitchell, *Gone with the Wind*, p. 35.

that it is somewhere in the southern United States, if not in Hollywood studios. The mansion carries the name of the place where Ireland began, but it is not that place itself.

35 | WHAT'S IN A NAME?

Very much like surnames, many Irish first names originate in or have a connection to the Irish language. Affection towards tradition is a lovely feature of the Irish character, and this includes names. If in many European countries old names, say from national folklore, are often a little bit out of fashion (you will hardly meet a Brit called *Beowulf* or a German woman called *Brunhilde*), Ireland is a bit more conservative in that regard. Many names of mythical heroes and great saints of old are still in use, and they obviously come from the Irish language.

Here is a maths puzzle for you. A school yard. Three in the afternoon. Parents have arrived to collect their lovely Oisín, Fionn, Fiachra, Niamh, Gráinne, Aoife and Méabh. How many girls and boys were collected from school today? Yes, traditional names from Irish mythology are quite unique. If you see or hear them for the first time, telling the boys' and girls' names apart might prove to be a bit more challenging than distinguishing John from Mary. But since you are not at school anymore, don't worry about your maths; I will just give you the answer: the first three names are for boys, the rest of them are for girls. P.S. If you are not sure how to pronounce a name, ask the owner instead of relying on your common sense; you might remember from previous chapters that Irish pronunciation is very special. Just a quick tip here: *ch* is always 'h', whereas *mh* and *bh*, of course, are pronuounced 'v'.

Apart from providing a link with Old Ireland, full of glorious heroes and no less glorious heroines, some of those names have beautiful hidden meanings which open up to those who know some Irish. A popular girls' name, *Aisling*, is an Irish word for 'dream'; another girls' name, *Fiona*, comes from *fionn*, which means 'fair, white' (the same word is used in Irish to say 'blonde'), while *Saoirse* is a proud woman's name meaning 'freedom'. The men's name *Rónán* is particularly curious – it means 'little seal' and is linked to an ancient legend about half-people half-seals (selkies).

Christianity, introduced to Ireland in 432, florished in the centuries that followed and produced great saints whose names have become popular ever since. You can guess the first one – Patrick, after the patron saint of Ireland. Ironically, neither St Patrick nor his name were Irish. He came from Britain, which was a part of the Roman Empire back then. His name had Roman roots and came from the Latin name *Patricius*. Most Irish saints were local, though, and usually had old Irish names like *Caoimhín* (Kevin), *Enda*, *Breandán*, *Ciarán*, *Aodhán* and *Ailbhe*. In case you were wondering: they are all male names except for Ailbhe.

This is all very well, but did the Irish call Patrick *Patrick*? Or *Patricius*? It is most likely that they called him *Pádraig*, the Irish version of the name. Where does 'Patrick' come from, then? Well, it is the anglicised version of Pádraig. Basically, the English did not content themselves with changing placenames. They did the same with people's names, making them look more English. *Pádraig* became Patrick, *Caoimhín* became Kevin, *Aodhán* – Aidan, *Breandán* – Brendan, *Orfhlaith* – Orla, and so on. Some of them managed to escape this butchery and stayed *Aisling* and *Aoife* and *Ciarán* and *Enda*.

However fond the Irish might have been of their native tradition, some common European names eventually arrived, together with the Anglo-Norman invaders at the end of the twelfth century. Being devout Christians, the medieval Irish were delighted to take such names as John, George, Catherine, Margaret, Peter, Paul, Thomas, Anne, Jane and so on. That is, names which have become popular all over Europe and beyond. The Irish, just like any other nation, pronounced and wrote those names in their own Irish way: *Seán, Seoirse, Caitlín, Mairéad, Peadar, Pól, Tomás, Áine* and *Sinéad*. Mary, another name popular all over Europe, received special treatment from the Irish. The girls were called *Máire*. However, the original bearer of the name, the Virgin Mary, was given a separate form, *Muire*, as a sign of respect. You can still see *Muire* on bilingual signs for Our Lady's school, church or hospital. The answer to someone's greeting in Irish, *God and Mary to you,* as you may remember, makes use of the same form: *Dia is Muire duit*.

Later on, the more anglicised Ireland grew, the more popular the English versions of these names became. Nowadays, it is all about your personal choice. You can use either an English or an Irish version of your name, if both exist. If you are feeling especially patriotic and would like to officially switch to the Irish version of your name (or indeed *vice versa*, if you think your parents were feeling too patriotic), you can get your name changed in your passport and, in case of the Irish version, enjoy the foreign border officer's facial expression when he sees something like *Séamus Ó Cathasaigh* (James Casey in his previous life).

However, I would say most people stick to the English version, often because they do not want to complicate their lives and the lives of all those admin staff, border officers and Starbucks baristas. This modesty on the border with embarrassement for these overly complicated Irish names seems to be of the same sort as the shame Irish people used to have for speaking Irish. Unfortunately, it is not just the name-bearer's embarrassment but the general assumption that if there is an English name let's go for that and not over-complicate things for no reason. You may find that even people in Irish administration sometimes get grumpy trying to type your name with endless *dh*'s and *bh*'s and *i*'s and *ao*'s. In many databases, including that of the shamrock-tailed *Aer Lingus*, fadas (the accent signs) are invalid characters, which turns a lovely Gaelic name into some kind of a lame hybrid.

And still, despite all this awkwardness, there is a name whose Irish version is way more popular in the country than its English counterpart. Just slow down for a sec and think: how many Johns have you met in Ireland? None? One? Two? That's right. There are some, but not as many as in England or the United States. What we have here in Ireland is *Seán*, which is sometimes compromised into the fadaless *Sean*. I am not sure why Seán is the chosen one but it may have originally been a half-conscious (or fully conscious) way for the Irish to distance themselves from England with its typical Johns. Whatever the reasons are, there is no escaping from Seán anymore, neither for the Irish nor, indeed, for the rest of the world. Seán is one of those Irish names which have spread quite a lot around the globe: *Sean Bean, Sean Penn, Sean Connery*. And this is not the only Irish name in Hollywood. On two recent occasions media correspondents from all over the world, as well as film-makers and Oscars hosts, were challenged to pronounce something a bit more complicated than *Seán*. An Irish actress, *Saoirse* Ronan, was nominated for an Oscar in 2007 and 2015 for her parts in *Atonement* and *Brooklyn* respectively.

Have you ever heard of an old Irish saint called *Mél*? No? Well, he was pretty important, a nephew of St Patrick himself! And the name has never lost that touch of fame as it is now securely linked to Hollywood through Mr Gibson. His mother was Irish and his father's grandmother too. Lots of Irish blood ensured his very saintly name. He is not simply Mel Gibson; his full name is *Mel Colmcille Gerard Gibson, Colmcille* being one of the most famous Irish saints, whose name, however, is not really given to the newly born anymore, Mel Gibson being an exception. His parents might have been going through that pang of nostalgia for good old Ireland when Mel was born, which led them down the Colmcille path. The Colmcille path, although unusual, is not as desperate as the Colleen path. What has *Colleen* got to do with it, you would say? A normal American name, leave it alone. Well, strictly speaking, it is not really a name. It comes from the Irish word *cailín,* meaning 'girl'. In Ireland, it has never been anything other than a way of saying 'girl' if you were speaking Irish. However, Irish emigrants, or maybe their children, stung by acute nostalgia, decided to call their newborn girls 'girl' in Irish. The trend seems to have started at the beginning of the twentieth century and produced quite a number of American and Australian Colleens (sometimes spelled *Colene* or *Collyn*).

IRISH AWAY FROM IRELAND | 36

Everyone is different in how they respond to nostalgia and their parents' or grandparents' heritage. Some go wild with their children's names, others turn to Irish language and culture. They get involved in organising Irish Studies programmes, teach, sow that seed of thirst for the Irish language in everyone who happens to be around – be they of Irish heritage or not.

Academic interest in Irish started at the end of the nineteenth century, and it was not confined to patriotic groups within Ireland. European scholars were fascinated by the language and the traditional way of life preserved by the Irish speakers of the West of Ireland. We hear of a Danish and an English scholar who came to the Great Blasket to improve their Irish, of a German academic as well as a bunch of Irish scholars and artists who visited the Aran Islands. So eager were they all to grasp the lifestyle and the language of the islands that the local people, instead of being struck by this interest, simply assumed that learning Irish was 'the chief preoccupation of the outside world' and, as documented by Synge, would with all seriousness say: 'Believe me there are few rich men now in the world who are not studying the Gaelic'.[42] People are good at getting used to the strangest of things, you know. That kind of attitude to international interest in Irish persists in the West nowadays. If I use Irish in

---

[42]   J.M. Synge, *The Aran Islands*, p. 39.

Dublin, people who don't know me will be amazed by the fact that I am from Moscow yet speak Irish, and for the fiftieth time I will tell the story of why and how it all happened (if you wake me up in the middle of the night, I will be able to tell you that in Irish no problem). However, when I go to the West, if they happen to ask me where I am from, not an eyebrow will be raised at the word *Moscow*; they will just nod and our conversation in Irish will resume as if no 'Where are you from?' diversion has never happened. They are right: it is normal to be studying Irish, it is no monster after all.

That academic nature of European interest in the Irish language and culture is well reflected in a number of Irish Studies programmes offered by several European universities. There is a strong tradition of Irish Studies in Germany and Poland. Another Irish hub is the Charles University in Prague. At least this is what you will read about in books and articles on Irish Studies in Europe. However, dare I say, they have overlooked something. You can argue about whether Moscow is in Europe or not, and where it is if it is not in Europe, but the fact remains – there is a sub-department of Celtic Studies at Moscow State University. Irish has been taught there since the 1980s after it was introduced by an Irish scholar, Garry Bannister (whose books on Irish are still on the shelves of bookshops here in Ireland). A small group of academics and their students really took to the language and were eager to study it on an extracurricular basis. As of 2002 it has been possible to minor in Irish and graduate as a linguist with your graduation paper written on some aspect of the Irish language (which I happily did). While Notre Dame University in the US boasts that it is the first US university to have launched a degree course in Irish Studies in 2012, Moscow is not far behind (ahead, actually): its first ever major in Irish Studies started off in 2010 and is offered once every five years now.

The academic interest that Europe has in Irish meets a more down-to-earth emigration tradition and nostalgia which sparked the presence of Irish in North America. You won't believe it but Irish was widely spoken in Newfoundland between the eighteenth and the beginning of the twentieth centuries. It was also a language of many early Irish immigrants in the US, to the extent that there were up to 70,000–80,000 Irish speakers in New York alone in the mid- to late nineteeth century[43] (they were not obliged to speak Irish there, note you, so it is likely that it was simply their native language which they continued to use in their new homes). They had their own Irish language newspaper, the first one of its kind in the world. Even though the number of Irish speakers in the US has significantly declined since then, according to the latest US census data of 2013 there still are around 20,590 people throughout the country who use Irish at home.[44] Not that bad actually.

This strong link with their Irish heritage, which thousands if not millions of Americans have, has led to the introduction of Irish or Irish Studies as a course at a number of universities, with the University of Notre

[43] R.H. Bayor and T. Meagher, *The New York Irish*, p. 274 (Google Books version used).
[44] Available on the website of the United States Census Bureau (www.census.gov) as an Excel document titled 'Detailed Languages Spoken at Home and Ability to Speak English for the Population 5 Years and Over: 2009–2013' in the data and tables section of the website.

Dame being the epicentre of Irish academic activity in the US. Many of these programmes are supported and funded by the Irish government, with study trips to Ireland and the Gaeltacht available to the students. Believe it or not, as of 2007, you don't even need to go to Ireland to find yourself in the Gaeltacht – haven't you heard they opened one in Canada? Yes, it is true, there is a Gaeltacht in Tamworth, Ontario. It is not your usual Gaeltacht though: Irish speakers do not live there permanently as a community. It is more of a space where people meet to speak Irish, organise events and attend summer schools. So, sorry, yes, you do need to go to Ireland to get that *Gaeltacht* Gaeltacht experience.

Other popular destinations for Irish emigrants – Australia and, obviously, Britain – do not seem to have a similarly lively link with the Irish language as the United States does. Yes, there were Irish speakers living there (and still are, in smaller numbers) but the Irish language has not really become *a thing*. There is an Irish course at Sydney University and quite a few British universities teach Irish Studies, but there seems to be less of a spark in relation to Irish. Why? Well, Australia is way too far away (why worry?) and Britain is right next door (fifty minutes away anyway). Just a wild guess.

IRISH GOES POLITICAL | 37

It seems that expats, academics and the curious public are not the only fans which Irish has secured worldwide. A couple of major political figures have recently turned to Irish in the hope of winning over the hearts of the Irish nation.

It all started with Barack Obama's visit to Ireland in May 2011. Apart from performing diplomatic duties, the American president had a personal reason to visit the country. It turns out that his great-great-great-grandfather came from County Tipperary in Ireland but left home for the United States during the Great Famine. In his speech in College Green in Dublin, Barack Obama focused on the shared history of the Irish and American nations and their determination to endure and overcome difficulties to achieve a better future. To emphasise that bond between the nations, as well as his own bond with Ireland, Barack Obama opted for a *cúpla focal Gaeilge*. He expressed his happiness to be in Ireland through Irish and called the people of Ireland his *cairde* ('friends' as you might have guessed). But the focal point of Obama's speech was the way he used the slogan of his 2008 election campaign. He wanted to reassure the Irish that they would get through the then current economic difficulties, so he repeated his famous 'Yes we can' phrase but this time it was in Irish – *Is féidir linn*. This very ordinary Irish phrase has really taken off since then. Magnets, postcards and T-shirts quickly spread across the tourist shops, displaying a photo of Barack Obama knocking back a pint of Guinness, with *Is féidir linn* running below the picture (see Picture 27).

The same year (and the same month!) another head of state, whose country has a much longer and more controversial relationship with Ireland, also turned to the Irish language to help bring down the barriers between the nations. England's Queen Elizabeth II visited Ireland in May 2011, marking the first British monarch's visit to the Republic of Ireland since it gained independence from the UK. Taking into account 800 years of a pretty tense (to put it mildly) and often bloody relationship between Ireland and Britain, you can imagine how much was at stake for both countries when Queen Elizabeth arrived in Ireland. Her message was that of reconciliation between the two nations. And what better way of expressing it than through the Irish language? Dublin Castle, a citadel of the British administration before independence, for the first time in history heard a British monarch speak words of Irish within its walls. During a state banquet in Dublin Castle the Queen gave a speech. She addressed the hosts in Irish: *A Uachtaráin, agus a chairde* – Madam President and friends. Impeccable in her famous English accent, the Queen also excelled at pronouncing the Irish *a chairde.* Many an Irish heart was touched by the gesture itself and the choice of words in the Queen's address, as well as the effort put into pronuncing those Irish words properly (it can be tricky, believe me!). However, the Queen's *cúpla focal* did not make any mugs or T-shirts – and rightly so, as the matter in question was much more sensitive and private.

Irish for Sale | 38

Listening to major politicians using *cúpla focal*, spotting Irish-sounding names in Hollywood or thinking of *the water of life* when buying a bottle of Jameson are nice but slightly impersonal ways of connecting with Irish. Nowadays, thanks to the tourist industry, every visitor to Ireland can hold a piece of Irish in their hands, buy it and bring back home. Just like that *Is féidir linn* magnet.

Alongside endless sheep, Guinness products and Celtic ornaments, the Irish language itself is being sold in souvenir shops. Door signs saying *Fáilte* ('Welcome'), shot glasses saying *Sláinte* ('Cheers'), keyrings naming family members in Irish, bags with bilingual captions, even tiny replicas of Dublin Buses with the destination *An Lár* ('The City Centre') are available to buy.

Unfortunately, some of the souvenirs turn out to be not as authentic as the manufacturers would like them to be. You do not need to look too far for the trouble-makers here – it is fadas, the little accents above the word. Their use does not always follow the rules, so you just have to remember which words need a fada and which don't. *If in doubt, leave them out* seems to be manufacturers' motto. As a result, there is a range of souvenirs which proudly display the warm Irish welcome *Céad Míle Fáilte*, or simply *Fáilte*, with the fadas missing (i.e. they say *Cead Mile Failte* or *Failte* instead). The Irish language it may be, but not as Irish as it could be. Anyway, if you are feeling particularly nerdy one day, go and inspect some souvenir shops and see how many missing fadas you can spot!

Sometimes, so as not to confuse our tourists too much with a completely different language, souvenir makers and other businesses borrow the Gaelic script and use it to write things in English to signal authenticity and attract tourists.[45] Check out the picture section for a pub sign inviting exhausted tourists to drop in (Picture 28). Using this script in English for decoration purposes has become such an established tradition that you may start to think it is simply an old English way of writing. But don't forget that appearances are deceptive, as you might remember from an earlier chapter. The Gaelic script was the main script used for handwriting and printing in Irish for centuries. It has retired now and is free to do all kinds of funny things, like getting hired by a different language.

Buying pieces of Irish is popular with tourists and locals alike. To bring a little bit of Irish into the everyday lives of local people, many bookshops sell Irish language and bilingual cards for various occasions. Homeware with Irish inscriptions are not a rarity in DIY shops. I don't know about you, but I am always welcomed into my in-laws' house by a lovely *Fáilte* door mat.

T-shirts with longer and more elaborate, often humorous, messages are sold by Irish language organisations like Conradh na Gaeilge's bookshop An Siopa Leabhar (as well as independent online shops). They mainly target that section of Irish society which

---

[45] This trick can also be used by non tourist-related businesses to emphasise the local character of their produce or services. Using the Gaelic script on English-language monuments and tombstones helps to add that extra layer of solemnity.

141

consists of people interested in Irish heritage including the language.[46] A lovely T-shirt was on sale in An Siopa Leabhar a while ago. Two beetles greet each other in Irish, in the traditional *God-be-to-you* way (I've told you about this before). The caption below the beetles is an Irish proverb which translates as 'one beetle will recognise another beetle', that is, to use the English idiom, *birds of a feather flock together* (see Picture 29). This T-shirt bursts with meaning: it uses some Irish, makes it funny by taking the proverb literally and also sends out a message about its owner's membership in the Irish-speaking community.

So indeed, isn't it time you picked up some Irish language tokens for your house? And if you are flying back home, or anywhere else really, keep an eye out for the green planes of *the Air Fleet,* known in Irish under the name of *Aer Lingus.*

SLÁN ANOIS!

---

[46] Such people who speak Irish and show an interest in Irish culture are called *gaeilgeoirí* (that is 'Irish speakers'). As a rule, this word is used in relation to people who live outside the Gaeltacht.

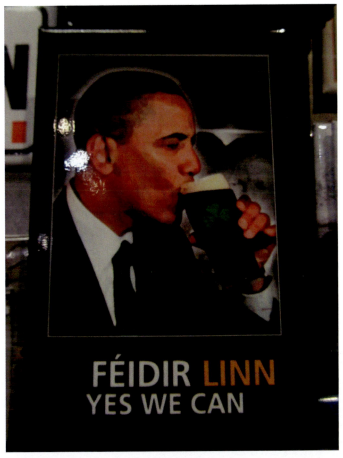

Picture 27

Picture 28

Picture 29

If You Want to Explore Further

Books with a Connection to Irish: Fiction and Non-Fiction

Friel, Brian, *Translations*, London: Faber, 1981.

Mac Murchaidh, Ciarán (ed.), *'Who Needs Irish?' Reflections on the Importance of the Irish Language Today*, Dublin: Veritas Publications, 2004.

McCaughan, Michael, *Coming Home: One Man's Return to the Irish Language*, Dublin: Gill Books, 2017.

Ní Dhuibhne, Éilís, *The Dancers Dancing*, Belfast: Blackstaff Press, 2007.

O'Crohan, Tomás, *The Islander: Complete and Unabridged*, Dublin: Gill Books, 2012.

O'Sullivan, Maurice, *Twenty Years A-Growing*, Oxford: Oxford University Press, 1983.

Sayers, Peig, *An Old Woman's Reflections*, Oxford: Oxford University Press, 2000.

Stoker, Bram, *The Snake's Pass*, Richmond, VA: Valancourt Books, 2006.

Synge, John M., *The Aran Islands*, London: Serif, 2008.

Films

Irish short films (both in English and in Irish with English subtitles): Available to watch in the 'shorts' section of the Irish Film Board at www.thisisirishfilm.ie.

In the Name of the Fada (2008): A comedy show about the complexities of the Irish language and ways of learning it.

Man of Aran (1934): A vision of traditional ways of life on the Aran Islands at the beginning of the twentieth century.

The Shore (2011): A poignant short film about leaving Ireland and coming back, betraying and forgiving. And love: for Ireland and each other.

The Song of the Sea (2015): An animated film available in English and Irish. It is a wonderful adaptation of one of the ancient Irish legends and a highly artistic and apt representation of Ireland – its landscape and its ways.

Yu Ming is Ainm Dom (2003): A hilarious short film which illustrates the gap between the official status of Irish and its everyday use in modern Irish society. Available on YouTube and the Irish Film Board website.

In Case You Decide to Learn Irish

AbairLeatOIDE is an Irish language learning app developed by Coláiste Lurgan in Connemara. It is available in the Apple and Google app stores and is a great resource for learning Irish and having fun at the same time.

Idhe, Thomas, et al., *Colloquial Irish: The Complete Course for Beginners*, London/New York: Routledge, 2008.

Ó Dónaill, Éamonn, *Gaeilge gan Stró! A Multimedia Irish Language Course for Adults*, Dublin: Gaelchultúr, 2010. (Available at beginner and lower intermediate levels.)

Ó Sé, Diarmuid, and Joseph Sheils, *Teach Yourself Irish,* London: Teach Yourself Books, 2003.

TEG Electronic Worksheets. These are free materials developed by Maynooth University to help candidates study for TEG – the international examination in Irish. The worksheets are available for levels A1–B2 in the teaching material section at www.teg.ie.

General Bibliography

Ahern, Cecilia, *The Marble Collector*, Dublin: Harper-Collins, 2015.

An Coimisinéir Teanga, *Official Languages Act: Guidebook*, second edition, 2003.

Ball, Martin J. and Nicole Müller (eds), *The Celtic Languages*, second edition, London: Routledge, 2010.

Bannister, Garry, *Proverbs in Irish*, Dublin: New Island, 2017.

Bayor, Ronald H. and T. Meagher, *The New York Irish*, Baltimore, MD: Johns Hopkins University Press, 1996.

Boland, Rosita, 'Broadside: Can Anybody Truthfully Say that Irish Is a Necessary Language?' *Irish Times*, 30 May 2016, available online: www.irishtimes.com/ life-and-style/people/broadside-can-anybody-truthfully-say-that-irish-is-a-necessary-language-1.2663495, last accessed 22 June 2017.

Campbell, George L. and Gareth King, *Compedium of the World's Languages*, London: Routledge, 2013.

Carew, Mairéad, *Tara: The Guidebook*, Dublin: The Discovery Programme: Centre for Archeology and Innovation Ireland, 2016.

Central Statistics Office, *Census 1926: Volume VIII – The Irish Language, with Special Tables for the Gaeltacht Areas*, Dublin: Central Statistics Office, available as

a pdf document online at: www.cso.ie/en/census/
censusvolumes1926to1991/historicalreports/
census1926reports/census1926volume8-irishlan-
guage/, last accessed 08 November 2016.

Central Statistics Office, *Census 2016 Summary Results
– Part 1*, Dublin: Central Statistics Office, 2017,
available as a pdf document online at: www.cso.ie/
en/csolatestnews/presspages/2017/census2016
summaryresults-part1, last accessed 05 June 2017.

Collins Irish Dictionary, London: Harper Collins, 2009.

Comrie, Bernard (ed.), *The World's Major Languages*,
second edition, Abington: Routledge, 2011.

Crystal, David, *An Encyclopedic Dictionary of Language
and Languages*, Oxford: Blackwell Publishers, 1992.

Darmody, Merike, and Tania Daly, *Attitudes towards
the Irish Language on the Island of Ireland*, Dublin:
The Economic and Social Research Institute, 2015.

De Fréine, Séamus, 'Dominance of the English
Language in the 19th Century' in D. Ó Muirithe
(ed.), *The English Language in Ireland*, pp. 71–87,
Cork: Mercier Press, 1978.

Dolan, Thomas P., *A Dictionary of Hiberno-English: The
Irish Use of English*, Dublin: Gill & Macmillan, 2006.

Doyle, Aidan, *A History of the Irish Language: From the
Norman Invasion to Independence*, Oxford: Oxford
University Press, 2015.

Fiontar Dictionary of Terminology: English–Irish, Donla
Uí Bhraonáin and Caoilfhionn Nic Pháidín (eds),
Dublin: Fiontar, 2000.

Friel, Brian, *Translations*, London: Faber, 1981.

Government of Ireland, *Bunreacht na hÉireann:
Constitution of Ireland*, Dublin: The Stationery
Office, available as a pdf document online at:

www.constitution.ie/Documents/Bhunreacht_ na_hEireann_web.pdf, last accessed 08 November 2016.

Government of Ireland, *The Official Languages Act 2003*, available as a pdf document online at: www. irishstatutebook.ie/eli/2003/act/32/enacted/en/ html, last accessed 08 November 2016.

Government of the United States, *Detailed Languages Spoken at Home and Ability to Speak English for the Population 5 Years and Over: 2009–2013*, United States Census Bureau, The American Community Survey, 2015, available online at: www.census.gov/ data/tables/2013/demo/2009-2013-lang-tables. html, last accessed 15 June 2017.

Hickey, R., *Irish English: History and Present-Day Forms*, Cambridge: Cambridge University Press, 2007.

Jaskuła, Krzysztof, *Ancient Sound Changes and Old Irish Phonology: Lublin Studies in Celtic Languages*, Volume 4, Lublin: Wydawnictwo KUL, 2006.

Kallen, Jeffrey L., 'English in Ireland', in Robert Burchfield (ed.), *The Cambridge History of the English Language, Volume 5 English in Britain and Overseas: Origins and Development*, pp. 148–196, Cambridge: Cambridge University Press, 1994.

MacConnell, Eoghan, 'Too Ridiculous to Be True? Dodgy Tattoo As Gaeilge Divides Internet', *Irish Independent*, 13 January 2017, available online at: www.independent.ie/entertainment/banter/ trending/too-ridiculous-to-be-true-dodgy-tattoo-as-gaeilge-divides-internet-35365643.html, last accessed 22 June 2017.

Mac Murchaidh, Ciarán (ed.), *'Who Needs Irish?' Reflections on the Importance of the Irish Language Today*, Dublin: Veritas Publications, 2004.

Maxwell, Constantia Elizabeth, *A History of Trinity College Dublin 1591–1892*, Dublin: The University Press, Trinity College, 1946.

McManus, Damian, 'Ogam: Archaizing, Orthography and the Authenticity of the Manuscript Key to the Alphabet', *Ériu*, 37, pp. 1–31, 1986.

Mitchell, Margaret, *Gone with the Wind*, London: Macmillan, 2014.

Mulryan, Peter, *The Whiskeys of Ireland*, Dublin: The O'Brien Press, 2016.

Ní Dhuibhne, Éilís, *The Dancers Dancing*, Belfast: Blackstaff Press, 2007.

Nic Pháidín, Caoilfhionn and Seán Ó Cearnaigh (eds), *A New View of the Irish Language*, Dublin: Cois Life, 2008.

O'Beirne Ranelagh, John, *A Short History of Ireland*, Cambridge: Cambridge University Press, 1983.

Ó Conchubhair, Brian (ed.), *Why Irish? Irish Language and Literature in Academia*, Galway: Arlen House, 2008.

Ó Doibhlin, Brendan, 'An Enterprise of the Spirit', in Ciarán Mac Murchaidh (ed.), *'Who Needs Irish'? Reflections on the Importance of the Irish Language Today*, pp. 140–158, Dublin: Veritas Publications, 2004.

Ó Dónaill, Éamonn, *Gramadach gan Stró!*, third edition, Dublin: Gaelchultúr, 2013.

Ó Murchú, Helen, *More Facts about Irish*, Volume 1, Dublin: European Bureau for Lesser-Used Languages, Irish Commitee, 2008.

Ó Murchú, Helen, *More Facts about Irish*, Volume 2, Dublin: Comhdháil Náisiúnta na Gaeilge, 2014.

Ó Riagáin, Padraig, *Language Policy and Social Reproduction: Ireland 1893–1993*, Oxford: Clarendon Press, 1997.

Oxford English Dictionary, second edition prepared by J.A. Simpson and E.S.C. Weiner, Oxford: Oxford University Press, 1989.

Reavey, Eugene, 'Head-to-Head: The Irish Language Debate', *University Times*, 21 February 2011, available online at: www.universitytimes.ie/2011/02/head-to-head-the-irish-language-debate,   last accessed 25 June 2017.

Sayers, Peig, *An Old Woman's Reflections*, Oxford: Oxford University Press, 2000.

Stenson, Nancy, *Basic Irish: A Grammar and Workbook*, London: Routledge, 2007.

Stoker, Bram, *The Snake's Pass*, Richmond, VA: Valancourt Books, 2006.

Synge, John M., *The Aran Islands*, London: Serif, 2008.

Wall, Maureen, 'The Decline of the Irish Language', in B. Ó Cuív (ed.), *A View of the Irish Language,* pp. 81–90, Dublin: The Stationery Office, 1969.

BIBLIOGRAPHY SOURCES AVAILABLE EXCLUSIVELY ONLINE

Celtic Inscribed Stones Project (CISP), University College London. The ogham stone database is available online at: www.ucl.ac.uk/archaeology/cisp/database, last accessed 18 June 2017.

Connemara Tourism, www.connemara.ie/en/content/connemara, last accessed 27 May 2017.

Daily Spud (a blog dedicated to all things potato), www.thedailyspud.com, last accessed 21 June 2017.

Daltaí na Gaeilge: Promoting and Teaching the Irish Language since 1981, http://daltai.com, last accessed 21 October 2016.

Ethnologue: Languages of the World, www.ethnologue. com, last accessed 21 October 2016.

Foras na Gaeilge, *Dictionary and Language Library*, www.teanglann.ie/en, last accessed 21 June 2017.

Foras na Gaeilge, *New English–Irish Dictionary*, www. focloir.ie, last accessed 21 June 2017.

GAA official website, www.gaa.ie, last accessed 25 June 2017.

Gaelchultúr, www.gaelchultur.com/Default.aspx, last accessed 27 May 2017.

Gaelport.com: Irish Langauge News and Information, www.gaelport.com, last accessed 21 October 2016.

Gaelscoileanna: official website, www.gaelscoileanna. ie, last accessed 23 June 2017.

Great Blasket Centre official website, http://blasket. ie/en/, last accessed 25 June 2017.

'Hollywood History', *The Hollywood Fair*, www.the hollywoodfair.com/history.html, last accessed 25 June 2017.

IrishCentral.com: An Irish-Americal Online Portal, www. irishcentral.com, last accessed 27 May 2017.

Logainm.ie: The Placenames Database of Ireland, www. logainm.ie/ga, last accessed 21 October 2016.

Numen: The Latin Lexicon, http://latinlexicon.org/ index.php, last accessed 25 June 2017.

Pilgrimage in Medieval Ireland, https://pilgrimage medievalireland.com/2012/09/05/medieval-pilgrimage-at-hollywood-co-wicklow, last accessed 14 April 2017.

TG4 official website, www.tg4.ie/ga, last accessed 25 June 2017.